THE CRUCIAL ENCOUNTER

THE CRUCIAL ENCOUNTER

The Personal Ministry of Jesus

by

LEONARD GRIFFITH

Minister of the City Temple, London

HODDER AND STOUGHTON

Printed and bound in Great Britain for
Hodder and Stoughton Limited,
St. Paul's House, Warwick Lane, London, E.C.4
by Cox & Wyman Limited, London
Fakenham and Reading

Published in Great Britain by Hodder and Stoughton
Ltd., and in Canada by The Ryerson Press, Toronto

Dedicated to
JAMES HUGH MACMILLAN, M.D., C.M.
HARRY ROY TELFORD MOUNT, M.B., M.S., F.A.C.S.
PERCY LAVERN BACKUS, M.D., C.M., D.P.M.

three Christian members of the
medical profession
whose patients will recognize them
in the pages of this book

CONTENTS

PREFACE

Too much religious literature is being written these days for the sceptics. Therefore I address this book not to people who ask, "Is Christianity true?" but to the reader who sincerely wants to know what light the Christian Faith sheds upon human problems and upon his problems in particular. Like most of my writings, *The Crucial Encounter* has grown from sermon material, and attempts, therefore, to speak to the needs of real people in real life in a real world. Such insights into human nature as I may possess derive not from a knowledge of psychology but from twenty years' experience as a pastor and spiritual counsellor. This is a book about the New Testament. Not that it makes an original contribution to the field of Biblical scholarship. I do not instruct the scholars; I learn from them and acknowledge my indebtedness to them. I take their powerful thought and, like a practical transformer, try to reduce it to a voltage which may light up a few ordinary lives. Behind my efforts lies the friendly encouragement and wise counsel of Mr. Leonard Cutts, Religious Book Editor of Hodder and Stoughton. Thanks are due also to my secretary, Winifred Haddon, and to other colleagues on the City Temple staff for their assistance in preparing the manuscript and in reading the proofs.

LEONARD GRIFFITH

INTRODUCTION

ONE aspect of the work of the historic Jesus which has not been sufficiently emphasized is the record of his personal ministry to individuals. We have so generalized the significance of his miracles and the application of his moral teaching as to forget that much of it was directed in the first instance not to mankind as a whole or even to the Church but to the individual.

It is important to recover this emphasis, because the individual seems almost to have lost his place in the total scheme of things. Modern life has become so mechanized, so organized and so standardized that man as a person is in danger of losing his significance. Politics, business, industry, science and culture have swallowed him up and made him a mere statistic, an object of general utility, reducing his personality from one to zero. In this situation it may well be that the bearded and sandalled beatnik is a more prophetic voice of God than organized religion, because while even the Church succumbs to the pattern of collectivism, the beatnik is at least saying, "I am human and I refuse to let you stereotype my life. Regard me as a person or not at all." The most healing word that the Church can speak to "organization man" is one that will restore his individuality and give him back a sense of his dignity and worth as a person.

To speak with any authority the Church must speak with the mind of Jesus. He was the loving concern of God in action. He believed, as no-one before him had ever believed, in the all-surpassing worth of the human soul. That belief shines in everything he says and does. It looks out from his eyes when they are happiest and when they are saddest, it trembles in the most loving consolations, it thunders in the most passionate rebukes that come from his lips. It is the inspiration at once of his pity and of his indignation. Jesus daringly taught that even the loftiest institutions and regulations of religion must take second place to the welfare of human personality. Indeed, so high does personality rate in the Divine scale of values that, like a shepherd leaving the rest of his flock while he searches for a single stray, so God is prepared to let the whole universe run itself while he seeks the salvation of one human soul.

The ministry of Jesus was pre-eminently a healing ministry; he came to make sick people well. If we study the Gospels, especially the one written by Luke, himself a doctor, we shall see Christ portrayed as the Great Physician who performed cures unknown to the medical science of those times. On the very day when he came into Galilee preaching the Gospel of God Jesus entered the synagogue at Capernaum and amazed the assembled worshippers by restoring sanity to a demented man. Later he went to the home of Peter, his first disciple, and by the touch of his hand raised Peter's mother-in-law from her sick-bed to fulness of health. That evening after sunset Peter's house became like the out-patients' department of a hospital, as the entire populace brought their sufferers and laid them at the feet of this Great Physician. So it continued throughout the days of his flesh. Across the pages of the Gospels there comes a procession of the blind, the cripples, the paralysed, the lepers and the insane whom Jesus healed by his miraculous power.

We reckon with only half the truth if we suppose that Jesus simply performed cures which any qualified doctor can now perform. In fact our Lord's healing ministry contained a dimension which science is only now beginning to recognize. The most revolutionary advance in modern medicine has to do not with drugs and operative techniques but with the rediscovery of the wholeness of human personality. For a time, in the fever of specialization, physicians and surgeons atomized their patients almost to a point of absurdity, provoking such amused questions as that which a wise old general practitioner addressed to a young doctor who announced his intention to specialize on the nose. "Which nostril, son?" he asked. But the situation is changing. More and more medical men are coming to realize that no organ of the body can be successfully treated in isolation and that often there is in organic illness some emotional or "spiritual" factor which must be dealt with before the patient can hope for a complete cure.

This new development has been given the rather formidable name of "psychosomatic medicine". It derives from two Greek words which mean simply "mind" and "body", and it works on the premise that the two are interdependent and that physical healing can only be partial unless it involves a treatment of the patient's whole personality. Whether a professing Christian or not, a doctor has only to read the Gospels with an open mind in order to recognize Jesus as the pioneer in psychosomatic medicine. The practitioner in any branch of medicine will profit by studying the techniques of Jesus, because in ministering to human ills he always treated the whole man, soul as well as body. Invariably his physical cures involved some kind of spiritual therapy. It might be the testing of the patient's faith or loyalty or gratitude or even his desire to be healed. Often he ignored the physical symptoms of a disease and went directly to its spiritual source. He never left a man well in body but unwell in soul. His constant question to men was, "Will you be made whole?"

That searching question, "Will you be made whole?" reveals the full scope of our Lord's healing ministry. It presupposes that health means the integration of all the divergent trends in our bodily, mental and spiritual life and that, therefore, the people who most need healing may be those who are not even aware that they are sick. Jesus directed a great part of his ministry to the "un-sick". He recognized illness in the very people who normally regarded themselves as models of good health. He once said sarcastically to the Pharisees,

"Those who are well have no need of a physician, but those who are sick," yet he left no doubt that he considered the Pharisees themselves to be far from well. To his penetrating vision sickness included not only blindness and paralysis and insanity; it included fear, materialism, depression, prejudice and all those abnormalities of the spirit which denied men fulness and happiness of life. He knew that any person, sound of body and sane in mind, could be afflicted by a moral malaise or a spiritual anaemia which, if not diagnosed and treated, might eventually result in severe suffering to himself and others. To such people as these Christ came as the Great Physician, the surgeon of their souls, drastically cutting away the cancerous cells of inner malignancy and giving them a health of outlook that restored them to wholeness of personality.

We are concerned with the *personal* ministry of Jesus and we must surely be impressed by its intensely personal character. Busy physician as he was, he never categorized his patients, treating them as mere "cases" to be dealt with by standardized therapy and techniques. He would have been shocked by the impersonal jargon that one hears in some hospital corridors which refers to patients not by their names but by their diseases. Jesus did not heal diseases; he healed people. In human need he always recognized a quality of uniqueness. He dealt with each "patient" individually, put his finger on the seat of that man's misery and suited his treatment to the specific case. Each man's illness, whether of the body or of the soul or of both, he diagnosed with unerring accuracy and for each prescribed the exact and appropriate cure.

It meant that every encounter with Jesus was a *crucial encounter*. Because this Great Physician possessed the penetrating vision and the healing power of God, no man or woman could come into his presence and be unaffected by it. Even today we have our different ways of reacting to a skilled and sympathetic physician. Some people flock to him eagerly, hoping against hope that he will diagnose their distress; they put themselves in his hands and trustfully submit to whatever treatment he recommends. Others come cautiously—"There's really nothing wrong with me, doctor. Just this little pain in my chest. Give me a few pills, and I'll be as good as new." Others keep far away from him because, having consulted him once, having learned the radical nature of their illness, they choose to go on living in misery rather than submit to radical cure. We see all these types in the procession that moves across the pages of the Gospels: Zacchaeus who gave away half of his goods to feed the poor; Nicodemus who would not recognize himself as his real problem; the Rich Young Ruler who turned away sorrowful, "for he had great possessions"; and a host of others whose lives could never be the same again after their crucial encounter with Jesus.

We must not read the Gospels in the past tense. To be sure, there once lived a man named Jesus of Nazareth who went about doing good. This same Jesus, however, because God raised him from the dead, lives for ever as the Physician of men's bodies and souls, performing even now the mighty works that he performed in Galilee and Judea long ago. The personal ministry of Jesus is a present reality. What he did for the sick and suffering in the days of his flesh he does here and now for all who are humble enough to receive him in faith. The Gospels contain no mere historical record of dead encounters; rather they offer to every man the present possibility of a living encounter with the Christ of God.

Helmut Thielicke tells that once he placed his little son before a large mirror. At first the boy did not recognize himself because he was still too young. He didn't know what a mirror was. He obviously enjoyed seeing the small image that smiled at him from the glass wall. Then, all of a sudden, the expression on his face changed as he began to see the similarity between his motions and those of the figure before him, and he seemed to be saying, "That's me!" The same thing, writes Thielicke, happens to us when we read the Gospel story with the eyes of faith. At first we listen to it as though it were an interesting tale with which we ourselves have nothing to do. Suddenly, however, we see ourselves in the Gospel mirror and we exclaim, "There I am, actually. This is I." We find ourselves reading the story in the first person; and because we identify ourselves with the people who surrounded Jesus and because we recognize ourselves in these people, we also recognize our Lord.*

This book is written with the hope that all who read it will recognize themselves in the characters whom Jesus encountered and helped during the course of his personal ministry to individuals. Somewhere in its pages the reader will find himself. He will know that the sickness diagnosed is *his* sickness. He will experience the crucial encounter with Christ and, hearing Christ's gracious offer, "Wilt thou be made whole?", he will reach out in faith to accept the gift of healing from the Great Physician of the soul.

* Helmut Thielicke, *The Waiting Father* (Harper and Brothers, New York, 1919), pp. 17–18.

CHAPTER I

WITH A WOMAN IN THE CROWD

ONE morning in June I sat on the western shore of the Sea of Galilee and looked across at the beige-coloured Gadarene Hills enveloped in a heat haze. That afternoon I journeyed northward along the shore to the ancient ruins of Capernaum, the once-bustling city that Jesus made the centre of his Galilean ministry. In imagination I joined the multitude that waited eagerly for the little fishing-boat bringing him and his disciples back across the water. I could hear the shout that heralded his arrival and feel the tense expectancy all around as he stood on the shore and began to teach. Suddenly a man in deep distress broke it all up. Fighting his way through the crowd, he rushed up to Jesus and began pleading with him earnestly, "My little daughter is at the point of death. Come and lay your hands on her, so that she may be made well and live." Jesus, who always valued individuals more highly than congregations, turned from his marvellous teaching opportunity and went with the stricken father.

We follow him through the busy streets, surprised when he stops suddenly and asks, "Who touched my garment?" It seems almost a foolish question, and with the disciples we retort, "You see the crowd pressing around you, and yet you say, 'Who touched me?'" But Jesus is not thinking of the swarms of people packed like sardines on the street. Someone has *deliberately* touched him. Looking around, his eye lights upon a woman, kneeling at his feet, with terror and ecstasy written all over her face. Something tremendous has just happened to her, something which has momentarily drained Jesus of his healing power. With infinite compassion he looks

B

at the woman and, realizing what has happened, he speaks words of reassurance that heal her soul as well as her body. "Daughter, your faith has made you well; go in peace, and be healed of your disease."

Think about this nameless woman who lived and died in Capernaum nineteen hundred years ago. So far as Christians are concerned she belongs in the category of "Very Important Persons", more important than all the philosophers in Greece, more important than Caesar upon his imperial throne. The reason is that she met the historic Jesus. She saw the Word of God incarnate, she heard his voice, she touched his garments and she felt the power of God flow from his life into hers, curing her of an incurable disease. Like all the New Testament characters this woman has a universal, timeless quality. She mirrors human nature. All the elements of her crucial encounter with Jesus are symbolic of a great many people in our society today.

Notice, first, *her incurable illness*. Though all the Gospel writers tell her story, none specifies the nature of her disease beyond saying that she "had had a flow of blood for twelve years". Today she would undergo a hysterectomy, but such surgery was unknown in the time of our Lord. Women simply suffered; and any woman can imagine the extent of her suffering, the sheer inconvenience and embarrassment, the painfulness and the sense of despair as she felt her strength ebbing away. Her own physician had declared himself baffled by it, so she had tried another physician and another and another and had gone the whole round of the medical profession with no result but an accumulation of medical expenses which had taken her last penny and left her destitute. After twelve years of costly treatment her condition had steadily deteriorated, bringing her now to the point of sheer desperation.

It is a terrible thing to suffer from an incurable illness, one that should allow of a cure and which the doctors do their best to cure, but which only gets progressively worse. We all know people who have been afflicted in this way, and our hearts break with sympathy for them. I think of a comparatively young woman stricken with paralysis from her hips down. Apparently there is no organic reason why she should be in this helpless condition. Her case has never yet been diagnosed. Meanwhile her parents, who cannot afford it, have transported her to specialists and clinics all over the North American continent, each time hoping for a miracle and each time bringing themselves closer to the brink of financial ruin. Now, with most of their resources gone, the poor girl just lies at home, a bed-ridden invalid. The moment you enter her room you can feel the hopelessness of the situation.

Disease can be of the soul as well as of the body. There are many people walking around with soundness of limb who yet carry within themselves a deep-rooted malady that no earthly physician can cure. In his last book, published after his death, John Baillie said, "At least one phrase in the General Confession we can all make our own: 'There is no health in us.' We know that the world is sick and needs to be made whole." Is it not remarkable that so many secular writers, who have their finger on the pulse of our common life and who sense that something is radically wrong with the social organism, talk of it in terms of a "malaise" or a sickness? That was the indictment of Oswald Spengler in his *Decline of the West*. To Europe and America he said:

"You are dying. I see in you all the characteristic stigma of decay. I can prove to you that your great wealth and your great poverty, your capitalism and your socialism, your wars and your revolutions, your atheism and your pessimism and your cynicism, your immorality, your broken-down marriages, your birth-control, that is bleeding you from the bottom and killing you off at the top in the brains—I can prove to you that these were characteristic marks of the dying ages of ancient states—Alexandria and Greece and neurotic Rome."*

Leslie Weatherhead told me of an emotionally disturbed woman who travelled six thousand miles from the West Coast of the United States in order to be counselled by him for two periods of two hours in his home in England. The woman in the Gospel story exactly! A symbol of people so hopelessly sick inside that they will travel half way around the world and spend their last penny in order to find a cure. Not all have the wisdom to consult a skilled religious counsellor. Some surround themselves with grown-up toys, others learn to do the "Twist", others go on long journeys, others are for ever changing something—their job, their house, their country, their marriage partner—in the hope that each new change will bring happiness. But happiness eludes them. Deep down they feel disillusioned, discontented and depressed. Spiritually they are sick and they can find no cure.

Another thing to notice about the woman in the Gospel story is that *she had heard of Jesus*. The New Testament says "She had heard the reports about Jesus". What reports? Presumably the reports of what he had done for people like herself. Here in Capernaum they were talking about the paralytic who had been lowered through a roof by his four friends, about the man with the withered hand in the synagogue and about Matthew, the tax-collector, who had renounced his life of corruption for ever. This physician obviously possessed the power to make men whole. No sickness lay outside his competence; there were no wounds that would not submit to his healing. Perhaps, then, he could do something for her.

The spiritual sufferers in our society need to be told about Jesus. They do not need to be propagandized with theological

* Alfred A. Knopf, Inc., 1926. Allen & Unwin, London.

theories about him; they simply need to hear his name. But the trouble is that they never hear his name. Nobody ever mentions it except as a term of blasphemy. Daily they come into contact with Christians who meet them on every level except the level of things that really matter. Some years ago a stranger with whom I shook hands after a service pointed to one of my church officials and said, "I never guessed that he was a pillar in the church. When I came to this city he befriended me in business and extended to me the courtesy of his club. Why didn't he invite me to his church?" Well, the truth is that we have a natural reticence about our religion. We count it too intimate and personal to wear like an old school tie or a fraternity pin; and to talk about religion with strangers seems ill-mannered and presumptuous.

The Communists have no such reticence. You will find them everywhere, in buses and dockyards and pubs and universities and fashionable drawing-rooms, spreading their faith with a tireless zeal. They frankly propagandize. They have something to sell and they employ the most effective methods of salesmanship. They urge their ideology upon people, ignoring every protest, every insult, in the conviction that they hold in their hands the gift that people most desperately need. Communists believe passionately that the gospel of dialectical materialism proclaimed by Karl Marx contains the cure of all the world's ills and with messianic fervour they trumpet the reports of what that gospel has done for them and for others who have embraced it. Does that explain, perhaps, the phenomenal victories of Communism over Christianity in parts of the world today?

The late Dr. Sangster told of a minister from Leeds who was fulfilling an engagement in Plymouth. Late in the evening he decided to telephone his wife and, as he waited for the operator to thread the call through the various exchanges of the Midlands, supposing the line to be sealed, he murmured to himself a verse of a favourite hymn:

My knowledge of that life is small,
The eye of faith is dim;
But 'tis enough that Christ knows all
And I shall be with him.

Suddenly, from somewhere in the Midlands, a voice vibrant with sadness startled him by calling out over the line, "Say it again! Say it again!" The minister held the telephone more firmly and repeated the verse with immense earnestness. As he finished, the same piteous voice called back, "Thank you. Thank you."* It is a picture, said Dr. Sangster, of how God employs our witness. Many people, whose sickness of soul cries for a cure, would be ineffably blessed if someone simply mentioned in their hearing the healing name of Christ. Christ is no ideology. He does not have to be argued and propagandized and sold. He has only to be reported, for in his very name is the power of God unto salvation.

Something else to notice about this woman in the Gospel story is *the timidity of her approach to Jesus.* For some reason, shyness perhaps, she could not bring herself to make a formal appointment with the Divine Physician or even to approach him directly and tell him the facts of her case. If someone had said to her, "Of course Jesus can help you. Come along. I'll introduce you to him," she would have run away in the opposite direction as fast as her weak legs could carry her. She had heard of Christ, of what he had done for other people, and now she thought it possible that he might do something for her, but she must approach him in her own way and on her own terms. "If I touch even his garments," she said, "I shall be made well."

It would be tragic if the Church ever ceased to maintain in the "inner city" the type of ministry that represents the hem of Christ's garment. The local church in the

* W. E. Sangster, *The Craft of Sermon Illustration* (The Westminster Press, Philadelphia, 1950), p. 42.

suburban community represents the robe of Christ. It enfolds people, draws them in, wraps them around and gives them a sense of involvement and belonging. But not all people are prepared to be identified in this way. Many want to remain on the Church's periphery, and any glad-handed attempt to draw them in closer will simply frighten them away.

One of the pew stewards in a downtown New York church told me that he saw a stranger standing at the entrance of the church and apparently participating in the service of worship. He had seen this man on several Sundays and had noticed that he invariably took up the same position—a regular worshipper, but never advancing beyond the vestibule into the main body of the church. In Christian friendliness the sidesman approached him and said, "Let me take you to a seat." Whereupon the stranger turned tail, walked out of the building and never came back again. Relating the incident, the pew steward said to me, "I suppose I made a mistake. I should have left him alone. He didn't want to be drawn into the church." That was true. This man wanted to touch Christ, but only the hem of Christ's garment. Perhaps he said within himself, "If I touch even his garments, I shall be made whole."

The city church can perform no greater work for Christ than to hold before the passing multitudes the hem of his seamless dress. It will be a costly role to play because it yields no reward in terms of increased membership and additional revenues. It may conflict with the popular idea of a church as a comfortable religious club that exists for the benefit of its own few members. We cannot recall, however, that Christ was terribly concerned about the pious enclave securely ensconced in the sheepfold. He attached greater importance to the strays, the lost, the sick in society, and he taught us that these, because they are the chief object of God's concern, must also be the chief object of the Church's concern—people who, though they will not look directly into the face of Christ, may be willing to touch the hem of his garment.

Notice also about this woman in the Gospel story that *her own faith made her well*. She may have been superstitious to begin with. Perhaps she believed that Christ's garment had magic properties such as pious people have often claimed for clothing worn by the saints. Perhaps she was convinced of it when the feel of that rough cloth shocked her like an electric current and she felt the power surging through her with new vitality and strength. In her delirium she did not know what to believe. But then she found herself looking into the face of God, into eyes that were aflame with understanding and compassion, and she heard a heavenly voice telling her where the real secret of her healing lay, "Daughter, your faith has made you well; go in peace, and be healed of your disease."

Jesus often spoke these words in the course of his personal ministry. *He* was the Physician, *he* performed miracles, *he* made sick people well, but never without their co-operation. Always he renounced the glory and gave credit to the faith of those whom he helped. Faith was the one constant factor in all his mighty works, the one condition he made of those who sought from him the gift of healing. He did not ask that men be good or pious or committed to his way of life but he did ask that they believe in him and trust him to help them. Nor did he demand a large, robust, adventurous faith. Even a timid, tentative faith like that of the woman in the crowd, if it were humble and sincere, could open the door of a human life to his miraculous power. Driving home this truth, Jesus said to his disciples, "If you had faith as a grain of mustard seed, you could say to this sycamine tree, 'Be rooted up and be planted in the sea,' and it would obey you."

On our side faith is still the essential factor in our crucial encounter with God's Christ. The almighty power of God, visible in the personal ministry of Jesus, is still at our disposal, but unless we have faith, that power can no more be discharged into our lives than an electric current can be discharged into a non-conductor. Christ does not demand some dramatic Christian decision of those who seek to be made whole by him; he does not ask us to believe all that the theologians say about him or trust everything he says about himself or commit ourselves completely to his Galilean programme of life. Christ asks only that we touch the hem of his garment, expose our lives to his influence and give him the slightest chance to do for us what we cannot do for ourselves.

In one of his books J. S. Bonnell recalls that a few years ago a United States Secretary of Defence committed suicide in his hospital room. They found at his bedside a book by Sophocles, the tragic Greek poet. It was opened at a poem entitled "Ajax", a story of frustration, despair and self-destruction. Here is one verse from the chorus:

> *When reason's day*
> *Sets rayless—joyless—quenched in cold decay,*
> *Better to die and sleep*
> *The never-waking sleep, than linger on,*
> *And dare to live, when*
> *The soul's life is gone.*

Dr. Bonnell suggests that we cannot help speculating on the possible outcome of this man's life had another book been on that bedside table, open at words such as these "If God be for us, who can be against us? . . . Who shall separate us from the love of Christ? Shall tribulation, or distress, or persecution, or famine, or nakedness, or peril, or sword? . . . Nay, in all these things we are more than conquerors through him that loved us. For I am persuaded, that neither death, nor life, nor angels, nor principalities, nor powers, nor things present, nor things to come, nor height, nor depth, nor any other creature, shall be able to separate us from the love of God, which is in Christ Jesus our Lord."* We cannot help speculating that it might have tipped the scales in favour of life if this brilliant and tragic man had touched even the hem of Christ's garment.

> But warm, sweet, tender, even yet
>   A present help is He;
> And faith has still its Olivet,
>   And love its Galilee.
>
> The healing of His seamless dress
>   Is by our beds of pain;
> We touch Him in life's throng and press,
>   And we are whole again.

* *No Escape from Life* (Harper and Brothers, New York, 1958), pp. 113–15.

CHAPTER II

WITH A BLIND BEGGAR

In this chapter I propose to do a very bold thing and write about the effect of prayer upon healing. I must write about it because I have committed myself to a study of the personal ministry of Jesus which, as the Gospels clearly indicate, was pre-eminently a healing ministry. Indisputably Jesus made sick people well. Some of his cures concerned emotional disorders and have now become commonplace in the practice of psychological medicine. Others concerned organic diseases, untreatable by the medical practice of his day, and no word describes them but the word "miracle". Jesus pointed to these works of healing as a sign of his Messiahship. When John the Baptist, brooding in his prison cell, sent messengers with the rather pathetic question, "Are you he who is to come, or shall we look for another?", Jesus replied, "Tell John what you hear and see: the blind receive their sight and the lame walk, lepers are cleansed and the deaf hear, and the dead are raised up, and the poor have the good news preached to them."

Jesus committed the ministry of healing to his Church. When he commissioned the twelve disciples and later the seventy to publish abroad the good news of the Kingdom of God, he gave them authority and power to heal the sick and cure diseases. The *Acts of the Apostles* shows us the Lord's commission put into action. Written by Luke, himself a doctor, this gripping story of the young Church leaves no doubt that in the apostolic ministry the healing of the body was no less important than the salvation of the soul. Our own times have witnessed a re-awakening of this forgotten ministry. Even among the more scholarly and conservative branches of the Church one finds a growing recognition that for too long we have defaulted a cardinal function of our faith to "hot-gospellers", Roman Catholic miracle shrines and Christian Science. Leslie Weatherhead's book, *Psychology, Religion and Healing*,* contains a storehouse of authentic facts about the proliferation of Christian healing movements and shows unmistakably that even the most coldly scientific doctors appreciate in a new way the role that religion plays in the healing of man's whole personality. We are confronted not by a theory but by a fact, and we do not argue with a fact; we examine it.

At the outset I had better clarify my own position. I do not believe that God intended prayer to be a substitute for medical treatment. Yet, if I became ill, whatever the nature of my illness, I should pray without ceasing for the return of health, believing that through the resources of medical science and beyond the resources of medical science there is a healing energy supremely accessible to faith. I should pray, not as a measure of last resort, but because conscious communion with God is the normal habit of my daily life. Nor would my prayer be a frantic "S O S" message but a reasoned response to the personal ministry of Jesus in the Gospels. We shall examine one incident in that ministry which contained all the conditions essential to a miracle of healing.

Look at *the setting of the incident*. It took place in Jericho, the oldest city in the world, the city of palms that still seems like an oasis in the wilderness at the northern tip of the Dead Sea. Having steadfastly set his face towards Jerusalem, Jesus journeyed through Jericho on the way to the Cross. Some miraculous things occurred that day, among them the conversion of a chief tax-collector and the healing of a blind

* Hodder and Stoughton, London, 1951.

beggar named Bartimaeus. Jesus opened this man's eyes, released him from the prison-house of darkness and ushered him into the glorious world of light. In years to come, when Bartimaeus gazed upon the blue sky and the green leaves and the faces of friends, he would remember that he owed his awakened sight to the fact that once Jesus passed through Jericho.

I have visited Jericho and other sacred sites in the Holy Land. As I retraced the Master's steps in that unforgettable pilgrimage, one thought kept flooding my mind—This is the place where it happened, the whole drama of redemption that reached its climax on a skull-shaped hill and at an empty tomb. Here Jesus lived. His feet stood upon this very soil, his eyes saw these very scenes, his ears heard these very sounds. Other great world religions began with the ideas, the philosophies, the visions of men, but in the Holy Land we realize that we call ourselves Christians because of something that happened at this particular place on the earth's surface. Here the Word became flesh, here the eternal broke into time, here God passed by. For that reason I should pray, as Bartimaeus prayed, for a miracle of healing.

Emmanuel Kant, the German philosopher, wrote, "It is at once an absurd and presumptuous delusion to try by persistent importunity of prayer whether God might not be deflected from the path of his wisdom to provide some momentary advantage for us." For Kant that was a logical deduction. He conceived of God as Sovereign Law in the physical universe and in man's conscience; and if that exhausts the truth about God, then prayer of any kind were a pious pantomime. For my part, while filled with admiration for the philosophers, I take my stand on the theology of the Bible which calls God not "Law" but "Father". A Father is still sovereign. He still creates, still makes laws but he is not bound by them. The Sovereign Father God cares first of all for his children; and, as God, he is free in his over-ruling purpose of love to administer his laws for the sake of his children's well-being.

Yet my prayer for healing does not rise from a reasoned theology; rather it echoes the faith of blind Bartimaeus who asked his friends the cause of the commotion and, when he heard that Jesus of Nazareth was passing by, cried out, "Jesus, Son of David, have mercy on me!" That restricted term, "Son of David", showed that Bartimaeus had a quite imperfect conception of Jesus, but the blind man's faith made up a hundred times for his poor theology. Christ does not ask that we understand him. He asks only that we turn to him and believe that he can help us. This alone we know about God— that once he entered our human scene and passed by the very place where we are. Incarnate in the Man of Nazareth, God made our life his life, our peril his peril, our suffering his suffering. Therefore he knows and understands and cares; and as he then stretched out compassionate hands of healing to all who cried to him from the depths of their need, so now he will not be deaf to the earnest plea, "Jesus, Son of David, have mercy on me!"

Then we look at the fact that *Jesus called the blind man to approach him.* Commentators remind us that Jesus, like any distinguished rabbi, would be surrounded that day by disciples and followers who listened to his teaching as he walked along. The streets of Jericho would be lined with spectators, all eager and curious to catch a glimpse of the bold young Galilean who had dared to defy religious orthodoxy. Suddenly a wild shouting broke the stillness. It came from Bartimaeus, sitting by the northern gate of the city. Indignant cries of "Shut up!" tried to silence him. The crowds resented this rude interruption of the heavenly words that flowed from the teacher's lips. But the blind beggar refused to be silenced. This was his only chance to escape from the dungeon of darkness, and he would allow no-one to deprive him of it. "Son of David, have mercy on me!" he kept shouting. Then comes the remarkable feature of this incident. In the tenth chapter of Mark's Gospel we read that "Jesus stopped and said, 'Call him!'"

"Jesus stopped." What a world of truth those words contain. We can picture the striking contrast in that Jericho scene: on the one hand, a great multitude; on the other hand, a blind beggar, a cipher in the social scale. Yet for his sake Jesus stopped, turned from the multitude and riveted his attention on one lowly individual. It typifies the intensely personal character of our Lord's ministry. Jesus was always stopping to help individuals, always turning his attention from the many to the one. The ruler Jairus, pleading for his sick child, interrupted Jesus at the moment of a marvellous teaching opportunity. A great crowd had gathered at the lakeshore to hear him. It would be excusable if Jesus had said, "Not now. I have a sermon to preach. I'll come over to your house later." Instead, Jesus stopped. Visualizing that scene, we catch the moving eloquence of the simple statement, "He went with him."

The great obstacle that discourages our prayers is the fear that God may be too great, too busy running his universe to be aware of the needs of one individual. How can the God who controls the stars in their courses be concerned with the pain in the pit of my stomach? We forget that it is in such personal concern that God's greatness consists. "Great is our Lord and of great power," sang the Psalmist. Why? Because he that "telleth the number of the stars" is he that "healeth the broken in heart and bindeth up their wounds." Standing on the top of the Empire State Building in New York a man gazed down at the people on the pavement below, people who seemed like a mass of swarming insects. "I suppose that is how the world looks to God," he said. In Jesus, however, we see another picture, the picture of a God who stops and singles out from the mass of men one suffering soul. This action of Jesus is God's way of saying to the lowliest person, lost in the crowd and overwhelmed by the immensity of physical nature, "You count! I am concerned about you."

Not only did Jesus stop. He called the blind beggar to approach him. That justifies my petition for healing. I pray not on my own initiative but because God invites me to pray. Indeed, as I read the Bible in this faith, it becomes one continuous invitation to present my needs unto God, and I realize that failure to pray would be a failure to take God at his own Word. One of the stock stories about the American Presidency concerns the young political candidate who promised his local constituents, as he began his meteoric career, that if ever they needed his help they must not hesitate to call upon him. Years later in the White House he was on his way to a Cabinet meeting when he heard indirectly that one of his old school teachers, now retired and impoverished, was about to be evicted from her home. Promptly he cancelled the Cabinet meeting and all his engagements, boarded a train and went to the help of this woman for whom he cared deeply. "Why didn't you get in touch with me?" he asked her. "I couldn't bother the President," she replied. "You forget my promise," he said gently. God also has made his promise to us in our times of physical, mental and emotional weakness: "They that wait upon the Lord shall renew their strength." We were faithless to forget it.

There is also the fact that *Jesus asked Bartimaeus to state his case.* Each of our Lord's healing miracles contains at least one unique element, one distinctive feature that sets it apart from all the rest. It might be the technique that he employed or the therapy that he prescribed or some searching question that probed the sufferer's soul and laid bare the source of his sickness. When blind Bartimaeus, directed by friends, ran stumbling into the presence of Jesus, the Master said simply, "What do you want me to do for you?" It seems a senseless question. Surely the man's need was obvious. Anyone else would have said, "Poor fellow! You're blind. You want me to restore your sight." Yet Jesus never employed any technique of cure without a reason, and there must have been a very good reason why he asked the blind beggar, "What do you want me to do for you?"

Perhaps, as in other cases, he intended it to be an object lesson for the spectators and, indeed, for the generations to come. It may have been his way of teaching us to be explicit in our prayers. Many of our prayers are not explicit. We approach God too vaguely, too piously and ambiguously, hoping that somehow he will be impressed and get the point of what we are trying to say. But God does not respond to generalities. "What do you want me to do for you?" he asks. "Be precise. State your case. If you have persistent pain or an incurable illness, and you believe that only a miracle can save you, then for the sake of my love, ask me for a miracle, and don't stop asking!"

Some of us feel inhibited in our praying by what seems like a very noble deterrent—the reluctance to impose our will upon God. We believe that God, to use theological terms, is both omniscient and omnipotent. He knows all things and he can do all things and do them without our asking him. We believe that, whatever our need, God knows about it already and will do what is best for us. It is God's plan that either we shall recover from our illness or continue to suffer or even die, so why pray to him? Can our prayers prevail upon God to change his plans and deal differently than he might otherwise deal with us?

One preacher has suggested the answer in a memorable sermon entitled "Does God Read His Children's Mail?"* He refers to those immature parents who, because of a shameless curiosity or a morbid possessiveness or a hard emotional

* Frederick B. Speakman, *Love is Something You Do* (Fleming H. Revell Company, London, 1959), pp. 117 ff.

tyranny, will stoop to any guile to control their children and will even lift their personal letters from the desk drawer and read them. Now what if God, asks this preacher, is too much of a gentleman for that sort of thing? What if he is too honourable a Father ever to steam open some sealed flap of our thinking, ever to take some thin envelope of our minds and hold it up against the light of his eternal vigilance? What if God, even though he could, simply refuses to read our letters unless they bear his name and address? Jesus was trying to teach that lesson when he asked blind Bartimaeus in a voice that everyone could hear, "What do you want me to do for you?" I have heard that voice in the secret place of my own soul, almost as though God himself were saying, "Stop trying to be so pious in your prayers! Stop beating about the bush! Be specific and state your case! What precisely do you want me to do for you?"

The incident reaches its climax in the fact that *Jesus answered the blind man's prayer*. "Take heart, rise, he is calling you," said the by-standers. "Take heart! Cheer up!" That is all that most of us expect from our prayers—a boosting of our own morale. But Jesus brought more than cheer to this sick man, far more. He brought a new factor into the hopeless situation. He brought the healing power of God. To the question, "What do you want me to do for you?", Bartimaeus pleaded, "Master, let me receive my sight." Moved by his childlike trust, Jesus responded, "Go your way; your faith has made you well." "And immediately," writes Mark, "he received his sight and followed him on the way." *"Your faith has made you well." There* is the basis for my persistent prayer in time of illness—the stubborn belief, undergirded by the personal ministry of Jesus, that within or beyond the resources of medical science there is a Divine healing power supremely accessible to faith.

At this point the author usually begins to recite case-

histories, but they do not carry conviction unless they bear
witness to an experience of healing either in his own life or in
the life of someone he has been privileged to help. I must be
honest and say that never have I suffered a crippling illness
that surgery or medicine could not cure; nor, as one whose
ministry has followed the conventional pattern, have I consciously participated in what may be truly called an act of
"faith healing". I am profoundly impressed by the experience
of other people, by the record of scientifically-attested cures
which have taken place at Lourdes and by the procession of
"wounded spirits" who found healing under the ministry of
Dr. Weatherhead. My prayer, however, arises not from
second-hand experience but from my belief that Christ continues today the ministry which he started in Galilee and
Judea and that what he did for sufferers in the days of his
flesh, he can do for us here and now, if we come to him in
faith.

Such healing need not appear to be miraculous. It may take
place through the normal channels of medicine and surgery,
but I shall give God the praise for it because I believe that
all healing is Divine. Jesus performed "miraculous" cures
only because in his time doctors were scarce and possessed
limited knowledge. Today the healing power that was mediated through Jesus is being mediated mightily through competent physicians, especially through those who combine their
scientific skill with the spirit of the compassionate Christ.
Centuries before the Christian era a wise man wrote, "Honour
a physician according to thy need of him with the honours due
unto him, for verily the Lord hath created him. For from the
Most High cometh healing." Some of the greatest medical
men have shared that simple faith. I know a brilliant neuro-
surgeon who never enters the operating theatre without offering a prayer, dedicating to God the skilled and powerful hands
which he believes that God has given him. I know a distinguished psychiatrist who often tells a patient, "I cannot cure

you. God alone can make you well. He may use me as the instrument of his healing."

I believe, moreover, that for a very human reason my prayer will assist the process of healing. Carried to their logical extreme, the theories of Mary Baker Eddy would create an intolerable social situation, but the Christian Science practitioner stands on solid ground when he tries to alter a patient's mental attitude, supplanting his negative thoughts with positive ones, setting right his personal relationships and bringing him into harmony with God. It is demonstrably true that praying patients are better patients, more relaxed, more serene, more co-operative; and for this you need not take the word of a preacher. Let the doctors themselves speak. In one of his books J. S. Bonnell quotes three prominent physicians. First, Lord Horder, who wrote, "There is a very definite point of contact between religion and medicine." Then Dr. Hyslop, of Bethlem Hospital, who says concerning the therapies that counteract nervous diseases, "I would undoubtedly give first place to the simple habit of prayer." Finally, Dr. Alexis Carrel who said, "The calm engendered by prayer is a powerful aid to healing."*

When sickness strikes, I shall pray, not only for therapeutic reasons, but because I believe that God will answer my prayer and will heal me in the way that really matters. If it lies within his purpose, he will grant a miracle, as Jesus did to blind Bartimaeus; and the doctors will have to confess, as they have confessed before now, that a factor entered my case which medical science is not qualified to evaluate. If God leaves me afflicted, if I pray but still suffer pain of body or mind, God's strength will be made perfect in my weakness, and my own spirit will be strong in the hope that I can do more for God through illness than through health. If I die, my loved ones will not curse God but will know that our

* John Sutherland Bonnell, *The Practice and Power of Prayer* (The Westminster Press, Philadelphia, 1954), pp. 22–3.

prayers have been answered on a higher level than we expected. Because we pray in the faith of Christ and ask God
for complete healing of body, mind and spirit, we shall trust
him to answer our whole petition, if not within, then beyond
the bounds of earthly vision.

CHAPTER III

WITH A PARALYTIC

"And when Jesus saw their faith, he said to the paralytic, 'My son, your sins are forgiven.'" What a strange way to heal a sick man! How would the nurses in a hospital ward react today if a medical specialist walked up to the bed of a paralysed patient, placed his hand on the inert body, looked into the pleading eyes and said, "My son, your sins are forgiven"? They would think that the doctor himself should be a patient in another kind of hospital. Does he not realize that the man is physically ill? Try a new drug on him, perhaps, or surgery, or physiotherapy that might restore some movement to his lifeless limbs; but to talk to him about his soul and say, "My son, your sins are forgiven"—could anything be more ridiculous?

We had better try to reconstruct the original story. It was one of those memorable incidents in the personal ministry of Jesus, so memorable that three of the Gospel writers include it in their narratives. It is such a fascinating incident that it challenges our imagination to fill in some of the unrecorded details.

We don't know the patient's name, so we shall call him Simon. Simon had been paralysed as long as people could remember, a sort of first-century paraplegic, condemned to be carried about on a straw-filled pallet. He was a familiar sight around the town, down at the lake-shore, in the synagogue and at public functions. Whenever his pallet appeared, carried by loyal friends, a sigh of pity went up from the passers-by or the assembled congregation. Simon had clung desperately to hope of recovery, seeking an audience with every physician and faith-healer who came to Capernaum, but none had been able to do anything for him. Each time his hopes became fainter, until finally he accepted his fate and resigned himself to a life of infirmity.

One day four friends came bursting into his house. "Wonderful news, Simon!" they shouted. "You can be made to walk again! . . . Jesus of Nazareth . . . He's here in Capernaum . . . He performs miracles . . . He cured old Thomas and Johanna's grandson . . . He can do the same for you!" No response from Simon. Just the weary smile of a cynic learning about another faker, another charlatan who would mumble a few words over him, take his money and leave him in lower spirits than ever. But the friends could not contain their enthusiasm. "It doesn't matter what you think, Simon . . . This Jesus, he's at Peter's house now. The whole town is over there. We're taking you to him even if we have to break our way in!"

Apparently they had to do exactly that. When they reached the home of Peter they found it surrounded by a solid mob of sufferers. Even the most able-bodied could not break through that human barrier and reach the door, let alone four men burdened by a sick-bed. What were they to do? For a moment they surveyed the situation hopelessly, their spirits crushed by the "I told you so" look in Simon's eyes. Then one of them had an idea. The roof! It would be quick work to climb the outside stairs leading to it, remove some of the loosely-joined tiles and lower Simon right at the feet of the Great Physician. Can you not picture the amazement of the hushed crowd within the house when they heard this crumbling noise above them and found themselves suddenly staring up at the open sky, an amazement multiplied as a pallet bearing a sick man suddenly descended on their heads? But Jesus showed no surprise. He marvelled, we are told, at the ingenuity and stubborn faith of these four friends who so believed in his healing power that they would allow no obstacle to prevent their bringing a sick man into his presence. His great heart went out to them, for "when Jesus saw their faith, he said to the paralytic, 'My son, your sins are forgiven' ".

You can read the whole story for yourself. It is plainly recorded in three of the Gospels. One can only imagine it to be the subject of excited conversation about Capernaum for months and years afterwards. There would be no sceptical head-shaking, no doubting its truth, no attempt at psychological explanations. This thing had happened, witnessed by enough people to make it an historically-attested fact. Simon, whom everyone knew to be an incurable paralytic, had been brought into the presence of Jesus Christ and healed. Their incredulity of soul is contained in their own words, "We never saw anything like this."

Yet not all the spectators shared the general feeling of wonder and admiration. Some of those present took an exceedingly dim view of what had happened. These were the Pharisees, the watch-dogs of religious orthodoxy, who saw the whole incident as a case of rank, unadulterated blasphemy. Not that they begrudged the poor paralytic his miraculous cure. They had human feelings of pity. It was the technique of cure that sent their spiritual blood-pressure soaring to the sky. They said nothing at the time, but Jesus could read the thoughts behind their stony faces. So he turned to them and asked, "Why do you question thus in your hearts? Which is easier, to say to the paralytic, 'Your sins are forgiven', or to say, 'Rise, take up your pallet and walk'?" All that the Master did and said that day indicates very clearly that he recognized an organic relationship between the paralysis of Simon and his conscious or unconscious sense of sin.

There *was* such a relationship. It figured prominently in Simon's mind and it derived from two sources. First, his thinking would naturally be conditioned by the orthodox theology of the time. The Jews connected all suffering with wrong-doing. They argued inexorably that if a man suffered he must be a sinner. Recall how monotonously Job's "comforters" pressed that point. "Who ever perished being innocent?" they asked. The rabbis declared categorically, "There is no death without sin, and no pains without some transgression." Indeed, a man's suffering might be the consequence not of his own sin but of something he inherited or contracted because of the sin of others. Of another handicapped creature even the disciples innocently asked Jesus, "Rabbi, who sinned, this man or his parents, that he was born blind?"

It may be that Simon's own conscience agreed with the doctrine. Perhaps he had, in fact, committed some grave moral offence which in his mind entirely justified the supposed relationship between sin and suffering. At first he may have welcomed his paralysis as a means of atonement. He may even have induced it as a means of escaping the social consequences. After all, society cannot punish a paralysed man. But now he would have to be convinced of God's forgiveness. All the medical treatment in the world could not make him stand up and walk until someone persuaded him that he had paid the full penalty and that the Divine Judge had pardoned him. Jesus may not have believed this crude theology but he knew that Simon believed it. That explains his strange technique of cure, "My son, your sins are forgiven."

Yet is it so very strange? Whoever denies the possibility of an organic relationship between illness and guilt has simply not kept abreast of the developments in modern medicine. Doctors today treat man as a whole personality. Medical journals abound in case-histories of physical sufferings which had their roots in some spiritual cause, and foremost among these spiritual causes is the sense of guilt. One eminent physician states his conviction as the result of treating many patients, "Most of the causes of mental derangement of a functional type are due to a sense of guilt." The patient himself may not always be aware of this. His guilt may be a delayed reaction to circumstances which he cannot recall, because at the time he thought that he dealt with them, and they no longer trouble his conscious mind. In actual fact he did not deal with the situation. The memory of it lies deeply buried in his subconscious mind where it acts like a splinter embedded in the flesh, poisoning the healthy tissues and sending up an ugly pus. Only a competent psychiatrist may be able to help him, and the cure will be lengthy and difficult because it involves a painful probing of every hidden corner of the personality, a spiritual surgery that finally exposes the splinter and removes the source of misery.

One of the most dramatic cases of which I have read concerns a housewife who suffered from dreadful nightmares. As often as three times a week she wakened her family and the neighbours by her terrified screams. Always she had the same dream. She went to the bread-box, opened it and there saw a deadly snake coiled up and poised to strike. Doctors examined her but could find no reason for this mental disturbance. At length her husband spoke to their minister, a family friend. The minister candidly confessed that he felt unable to help because he had sensed a spiritual barrier between himself and this woman. However, he readily agreed to visit her and was not surprised when she said, "I'm afraid praying over me won't straighten things out." The minister promised that he had no intention of praying over her but he did ask some leading questions about snakes and their association in her mind. Finally it came out that years earlier she had been terrified by a real snake coiled at the mailbox of the rural home where she lived with her parents. She went daily to that mailbox for a reason. She had tried to forget it, but under the minister's gentle insistence she poured out her confession with a flood of tears. Secretly she had been in love with her sister's fiancé, an American soldier fighting in the Korean War. Regularly she stole the letters which he wrote to her sister, read them and destroyed them in the hope that her sister would forget about him and fall in love with someone else. He came home, however, and married her sister; and this woman, secure in her own life, drove the deception from her mind. Then her brother-in-law died suddenly, and that was when the nightmares began—symptoms of the buried splinter of guilt which could only be removed by begging forgiveness of her own husband, her bereaved sister and God.*

I purposely refrain from citing cases of organic illness which have been proved to be rooted in the sense of sin; and I do so because I cannot claim to have been personally involved in such a case. As a spiritual counsellor, however, I have tried to help many people whose nervous ailments such as insomnia, palpitation, fainting spells and migraine headaches were unquestionably due to suppressed guilt feelings. Scientists tell us that one of the major problems connected with the development of atomic energy has to do with the disposal of atomic garbage. Apparently you cannot employ fissionable material for war or peace without producing vast quantities of lethal radioactive waste. One means of disposal is to seal the waste in cement blocks and sink them in the deepest part of the ocean. Sometimes, however, the pressure of gas cracks these containers, and the gas rises to the surface as a poisonous influence. This scientific fact finds a parallel in personality. We can treat the emotional disturbances that rise to the surface of the mind but we can treat them only as symptoms, because deep below the surface lies their poisonous source which has to be exposed and dealt with before there can be any hope of a complete cure.

Even inherited guilt turns some people into neurotics. Whether transmitted by the genes or by the emotional environment or by both we do not know, but we do know that it can be devastatingly real. One of the unhappiest of men was Soren Kierkegaard, the great Danish theologian, who squandered his youth in dissolute living and lost his brief manhood in the self-torture of a gloomy, ascetic religion. For this he blamed his father who communicated to him, even as a child, a joyless religion coloured by the sense of guilt. It seems that the older man never stopped brooding over two traumatic experiences in his life. His boyhood had been one

* "The Splinter of Guilt," by Arthur Gordon, published in *Guideposts*, April 1962.

of poverty and hardship. One day, herding sheep on a barren heath of Jutland, in loneliness, misery and futile rebellion, he lifted his face to a pitiless sky and cursed God. Never could he forget this. More tangible, and weighing even more heavily upon his conscience, was the sin of sexual incontinence after the death of his first wife. Before the year of mourning was over he married his housekeeper, and five months later she gave birth to a child. The elder Kierkegaard never forgave himself. He felt that a curse lay upon his life and, whether consciously or not, he bequeathed that curse to his brilliant son. Mightily and marvellously God used Soren Kierkegaard and spoke through him a Word which has become the basis of much modern theology, but he himself wrote out of deep melancholy, out of a sickness of soul which he never ceased to attribute to the guilt-ridden influence of his father.

So we come back to the first-century paralytic whom we now recognize not as an ancient figure but as a very modern one with whom, perhaps, we may even identify ourselves. Guilt may or may not have actually triggered off the cerebral haemorrhage that caused his paralysis, but the fact remains that, conditioned by the thinking of his day, he possessed a very real sense of guilt that became part of his total illness. To this spiritual condition Jesus directed his powers of healing because he knew that, whatever might be done for the crippled body, the man himself could never be healed until his soul was at peace with God. Even had Jesus left him a cripple and simply mediated God's forgiveness he would have answered the deeper need.

We return also to the scandalized Pharisees. "It is blasphemy!" they exploded, "Who can forgive sins but God alone?" They were right. Only God *can* forgive sins, but what God alone can do Jesus *did* there and then. Sensing their hostility, Jesus joined issue with them on their own ground. Since they believed that a sick man must be a sinner and could not be cured until God forgave his sins, surely they would be convinced that whoever possessed God's power to heal a sick man possessed also God's power to forgive him. "You don't believe me," Jesus said, in effect, "then watch this." He turned to the paralytic. "I say to you, rise, take up your pallet and go home." "And he rose," writes Mark in his Gospel, "and immediately took up the pallet and went out before them all; so that they were all amazed and glorified God, saying, 'We never saw anything like this!'"

This miracle of healing did not convince the Pharisees, of course; it only humiliated them and hardened their opposition to Jesus. More than anything else, however, the power of Jesus to forgive sins kindled within his own followers the burning conviction that he was indeed the Christ, the Son of God. They tried to explain him by lesser categories—leader, teacher, priest, prophet—but none was big enough to contain him. Again and again men recognized in Jesus the power which belonged only to God. They found that he could do for them what the prophets had foretold that only God could do. They marvelled at his mastery over nature, disease, insanity and death, but chiefly at his mastery over evil. Across the pages of the Gospels there walks a procession of depraved, degraded, despised men and women, their souls stained by sin, who passed beneath his healing shadow and emerged into the clear, clean light of purity and goodness and self-respect.

The point of this incident, however, and of all the incidents in the Gospel narrative is not what Jesus *did* but what he *does* for men and women paralysed by the sense of sin. Still he removes from the soul that splinter of guilt which deranges the mind, disturbs the emotions and even diseases the body. Those who come trustfully to God in the name of Christ can still hear the gracious words, "My son, your sins are forgiven." Of course, we shall be reminded that modern man is no longer worried about his sins. Reinhold Niebuhr quotes a popular writer who dismisses the sense of sin as "a psychopathic aspect of adolescent mentality". The utterance comes, he says, from "a particularly vapid modern social scientist". To sneer at sin may indeed represent a knowledge of social science but it represents also an abysmal ignorance of human nature.

Some months ago I spoke at a conference of sixth-formers who came from a number of North London secondary schools. Among the questions submitted to me was this one: "If you don't believe in God, but are still sorry for your sins, will you be forgiven?" You can anticipate my answer. I said, "This question contradicts itself. If you don't believe in God, how can you talk about sin? Sin is a religious word. It means disobedience against God. Or, suppose you call it moral failure, from whom do you want forgiveness, if you don't believe in God?" Yet I welcomed the question not only because it revealed a religious instinct in these young people, many of whom came from unreligious homes, but because it revealed that the sense of sin is a moral fact that we cannot argue away and still live in a world of moral realities. Any man with any sense of moral responsibility will be more troubled about his misdeeds and failures than about anything else in the world. Nor can he, as a moralist, forgive himself, precisely because he is a moralist. He knows that forgiveness has to come from beyond himself, and ultimately this compels belief in God. To bring God into the picture makes the situation worse, because then the sense of moral failure becomes something more serious, a sense of sin against God. But it also makes the situation better, because a new possibility comes into view, the possibility of God's forgiveness. This is more than a possibility. It is a reality made visible in the personal ministry of Jesus who came to show us what God is like, a God who looks compassionately at the most sinful soul, paralysed by self-loathing, and says with infinite compassion, "My son, your sins are forgiven."

Therefore, it may well be that the man lying in a modern hospital ward will not be healed of his physical illness until some physician does look into his pleading eyes and says, "My son, your sins are forgiven." Perhaps *we* shall never be healed of our emotional disorders until we hear a voice speaking in our own conscience those same words of absolution. So let me be specific and very personal. Let me ask you to go down into the secret place of your heart. Unlock the hidden door. Take out the unresolved guilt. It may be something that you have tried to forget—a fleeting love-affair, the neglect of your parents before they died, an act of childish revenge, your failure to serve sacrificially in some great cause. Take out the memory and lay it at the feet of the forgiving Christ. I cannot promise you immediate health of body and mind but I can promise that you will have taken the decisive step towards wholeness of personality.

CHAPTER IV

WITH A DANGEROUS DEMONIAC

THE treatment of illness frequently includes some form of therapy. Indeed, it is the therapy that consolidates the cure and makes it complete. After his operation a cancer patient may have to undergo a series of distressing deep X-ray treatments in order that the last traces of malignancy may be destroyed. The accident victim, when his fractured bones have knitted, must exercise his limbs, painfully perhaps, to restore their full mobility. The mental patient, after shock treatments and lengthy analysis, will be given certain occupational tasks as a means of gradual rehabilitation. In many cases the onus of responsibility rests on the patient himself. After doing everything within his skill the surgeon or physician says, in effect, "Now it's up to you. If you want to be completely well, this is what you have to do."

That was a cardinal feature in the personal ministry of Jesus. Always he healed the whole personality, and to this end he often followed a cure by prescribing a kind of therapy, some act or series of acts which the patient himself must perform in order to be completely well in body, mind and spirit. We see an example of this in one of his most convulsive healing miracles, a cure so unforgettable that three of the Gospel writers include it in their narratives.

Exhausted after a long day of teaching, Jesus and the disciples sought solitude by boarding a small fishing-boat and crossing the Sea of Galilee. Suddenly a wind swept down from the surrounding hills, stirring up waves so high and rough that they tossed the little craft crazily about in the pitch darkness, threatening to smash it in splinters and send the sailors to a watery grave. Panic-stricken, the disciples awakened Jesus who was sleeping in the stern as peacefully as a child. He rebuked them for their lack of faith; then he rebuked the storm, "Peace! Be still!" "And the wind ceased," we are told, "and there was a great calm." As dawn broke, they approached the Gadarene Hills and stepped on the eastern shore only to be met by a human animal, a man more terrifying than any storm, a raving lunatic who found his asylum among the tombs of the dead.

There are four moments in this crucial encounter as Mark describes it in the fifth chapter of his Gospel. First, the confrontation itself, which must have been frightening to behold. This man was a maniac, so dangerous that today we should bind him in a straitjacket and lock him in a padded cell. Indeed he had been chained many times but by his superhuman strength he had torn his iron fetters to shreds, so that no-one dared to come near him. You can visualize this naked, insane creature, crouched like a wild beast at bay, ready to spring for the kill. You can smell the fear of the disciples as they slowly edged back towards the boat. And you can see Jesus, who had subdued the forces of physical nature, calmly facing the unbridled forces of demented human nature. It was a prefiguration of the Cross—the raging strength of man confronted by the quiet strength of God.

The second moment in this crucial encounter is the actual cure. Jesus performed it by a strange technique. To heal the madman he caused a herd of two thousand pigs to go berserk and stampede down the steep cliffs into the lake where they were drowned. It seems unhumane until you remember that eventually they would have been slaughtered anyway and that a few breakfast tables without bacon were small enough price to pay for a man's sanity. In those days it was believed that a person was insane because demons dwelt within him. Jesus may not have believed this primitive doctrine, but the Gadarene demoniac certainly believed it and he could never be

C

cured until he saw with his own eyes that the legion of demons had left his body and found another dwelling in the bodies of men or animals. We can only imagine that, as the last animal sank beneath the water, the demoniac sank to his knees in grateful self-consciousness that he had ceased to be an animal and had again become a man.

In the third moment we see the hostility of the citizens. Dismayed by the loss of the swine, the herdsmen rushed into the city to exonerate themselves and to explain what had happened. Before long they reappeared, presumably with the owners who looked at the vacant hilltop and then at the former demoniac, now clothed and composed and conversing quietly with Jesus and the disciples. Did they shout for joy that a fellow-citizen had been raised from a living death? Did they thank his healer and take him back to the town in triumph? Not for a moment! Mark tells us that "they began to beg Jesus to depart from their neighbourhood"—ten words that can be reduced to two: "Get out!" It was their way of saying, "You value men, we value pigs, so leave our country before you do further damage to our economy!"

The fourth moment is that of a brief dialogue between patient and physician. As Jesus and the disciples, threatened by the indignant citizens, stepped into their boat, the man rushed up and begged to be taken with them. This was not unusual. Other sufferers, like Blind Bartimaeus, followed Jesus after he had given them back their health. Besides, what else could the former demoniac do? His family had probably written him off as dead. He would always be stigmatized for having been mentally ill. People would regard him suspiciously and whisper, as people do, "He's not quite right, you know." Worst of all, the angry glares of his townsfolk told him eloquently that he would not be forgiven for the loss of the pigs. Yet Jesus denied his request. Heartless as it seems, he instructed the man to do the most difficult thing possible. "Go home to your friends," he said, "and tell them how much the Lord has done for you and how he has had mercy on you."

Here is the distinctive feature in this crucial encounter, the feature which compels our attention because it still figures prominently in our own encounter with God's Christ. Why did Jesus refuse the man's request? Putting pity aside, would not the Master have strengthened his own influence by including in his entourage a living testimony to his power over demons? Surely the cured demoniac, in constant companionship with Christ, would have become an ardent and devoted disciple, his witness infinitely more convincing than that of Matthew captured from the seat of corruption or Peter redeemed only from a sense of guilt. Yet we know that the Great Physician never employed a technique of cure without a reason, and there must have been a very decisive reason for excluding this man from the apostolic group and sending him back to bear witness in the hostile environment of his familiar and accustomed world.

It was the Great Physician's way of prescribing a therapy. To be sure, he had administered the healing shock treatment, ostensibly curing the patient, but that was not enough. Jesus knew very well that, in order to consolidate the cure and prevent all possibility of regression, the patient must himself carry through a painful but vitally essential process of therapy. This would not be accomplished if he became a member of the apostolic community. Some sufferers might benefit by staying at their healer's side and following him across new frontiers, but for the cured demoniac this would be the worst thing that he could do. The very nature of his illness had cut him off from his familiar world, so that what he most needed was not to escape from that world but to return to it and rehabilitate himself in it. Strangers in other parts of the country would certainly be impressed by the story of his miraculous cure, but for his own sake he needed to tell that story again and again to the very people who pigeon-holed him in their minds as a lunatic. This was his therapy, the difficult thing that he must do; without it his cure could not be complete.

You may have seen the popular musical play, based on fact, about an attractive young girl who became a postulant in a Roman Catholic convent. Loving her, but doubting her temperamental suitability for the cloistered life, the Mother Superior sent her away for a season to serve as housekeeper to a handsome widower with a large family. Gradually this girl won the hearts of all the children and one day, to her utter consternation, she realized that she had also won the heart of their father and that she was in love with him. At once she returned to the convent and offered to take her vows, but the wise Mother Superior saw through her dilemma and refused to accept her. "Religion is not an escape from reality," she told the girl. "You have your problem out in the world. You must go back to face it."

Jesus said that to the demoniac and he says it to every man whom he truly encounters in an experience of spiritual healing. When first we become Christians, when first the transforming power of Christ floods our lives, we have the natural impulse to keep life fixed at that emotional point. We want to climb into the fishing-boat. We want to stay with Jesus permanently. We want to make a full-time business of being religious, enter a monastery, perhaps, become priests or pastors or simply warm ourselves in the holy huddle of the Church. To do so, however, would not strengthen but weaken our fellowship with Christ, for then we should be making our religion a retreat from reality. Jesus does call some to bear witness within the Church. Most of us, however, he sends back to our familiar world, our home, office, workshop, classroom, community, and he instructs us to talk about him to the people who knew us before we took a religious word on our lips, the people who will be least impressed and who will perhaps resent and ridicule our Christian witness. That is our therapy, essential to consolidate our crucial encounter with Christ and make it complete.

If we take seriously this feature of our crucial encounter with Christ we shall radically revise our image of the Church.

What, in fact, is the image now popularly held? It would not be incorrect to say that many people visualize the Church as a kind of religious theatre. In tangible terms they see it as an impressive building where one or two performances take place every Sunday. They believe that no effort, no expense must be spared to make the performance professionally perfect. The scenery, the lighting, the music, the pageantry and the spoken word must please the audience and must be designed to attract the largest possible audience. Indeed, the size of the audience determines the show's success; it may even determine how long a particular show will run.

What a vastly different image of the Church emerges from the personal ministry of Jesus! He and his followers never thought of constructing impressive buildings and promoting religious shows because they were too busy constructing Christian character and promoting the Kingdom of God. Jesus saw the Church not as an audience of spectators watching a performance but as an army of soldiers assaulting the evils of society and capturing the hearts of men. He did not call disciples. He called apostles and, though he occasionally took them aside for seasons of prayer and worship, it was only to instruct and fortify them, so that they might go back into the world's warfare better equipped to perform their demanding and dangerous duties. His last words, recorded not in the Gospels but in the *Acts of the Apostles*, constitute the Church not into a monastic community but into a witness society charged with proclaiming the good news "in Jerusalem and in all Judea and in Samaria and to the end of the earth".

One of the healthiest by-products of the decline of church-going in Britain is that we have been forced to re-cast our image of the Church. Naturally we deplore this evident decline, and some older people look back nostalgically to the days that preceded the First World War when Sunday was a Sabbath and our great sanctuaries overflowed with eager worshippers. "If only it could happen again," we murmur. "If only we could persuade people to come into the churches, then we should see the revival of spiritual values desperately needed in our society." But is that the answer?

We had better be realistic and face the fact that in our generation the Church is not a crowd of people pouring into a shrine to make up an audience for a popular preacher or a recital of sacred music. In our generation the Church is a small company of Christian soldiers trickling out of the shrine to fight the battles of the Kingdom of God where men live and work and play and make decisions. In a lecture delivered at the City Temple in November 1963, Dr. Thomas Jessop, one of Britain's leading philosophers, said, "We shall not persuade a nation that has become widely secularized in two generations to put its affairs into a deeply decent order (still less convert it to our faith) by merely talking at it from self-enclosed sanctuaries. Our doors must be open as much to let folk out as to let them in . . ."

If we take seriously this feature of our crucial encounter with Christ we shall also radically revise our image of the Christian layman. The Church has yet to define what is meant by a good layman. Too many of us cling to the conservative tendency that estimates a Christian's value by the amount of time that he or she spends on church premises. We refuse to let go the image of the layman as a minister's unpaid assistant who busies himself with running the internal machinery of a church. Indeed, once having brought a man inside the fellowship of Christ, we have a pathological fear that we shall fail him unless we put him to work immediately and give him something useful to do. The truth is that often we fail him *because* we give him something to do. This man may already be carrying a heavy burden of vocational, family or social responsibility; and adding to that burden will not strengthen his devotion to Christ but only weaken it by giving him a sense of guilt.

Sitting at a hospital snack-bar one day, I sniffed the unmistakable smell of anaesthetic. A clever surgeon clothed in white sat on the chair beside me, exchanged a few pleasantries, and said, "I'm afraid I can't be at the Board meeting tonight. I have two operations booked, I must drop in on some of my other patients, and it will be at least nine o'clock before I can get away from the hospital." He toyed with his cup of coffee, then added, "I have been thinking about this business of holding office in the Church. I really can't give it the time that it deserves. I ought to resign."

What could I say to such a man, a superb Christian, utterly dedicated to the ministry of healing which he performed with the skill and in the spirit of Christ? What would Jesus have said to him? He would have said, "Go home to your operating theatre and do the Church's work there. I have other servants without your skill and without your opportunities who are well qualified to run the internal affairs of my Church. You have been called and equipped to bear your witness out in the world where you live and work." Christ says that to many a man in his crucial encounter; and the Church only frustrates Christ's purpose for that man by siphoning off time and energies that were better deployed in those areas of the world's life where he can have a special influence. Perhaps the Second Assembly of the World Council of Churches gave us a new image of the Christian layman when it said that "the real battles of the faith are being fought in factories, shops, offices and farms, in political parties and government agencies, in countless homes, in the Press, radio and television, in the relationship of nations." Who is the good layman? Not a stage-hand in a religious theatre but a Christian soldier fighting on the front-line of life.

We should still prefer, of course, to climb into the fishing-boat. It is so much easier to confine one's religion to a sacred building and an hour on Sunday and to feel that one's Christian responsibility can, in fact, be discharged within the "holy huddle" of the Church. We all shrink from advertising our religious convictions at home or at work or in the circle of our friends, a reticence which, curiously enough, does not extend to our political or social convictions. Jesus knew from his own bitter experience at Nazareth that he was prescribing no easy therapy for his patient when he instructed him, "Go home to your friends and tell them how much the Lord has done for you." But why *tell* his friends? Why not let his own transformed life speak for itself? Why? Because no life, however Christian, is good enough to speak for Christ. If Christ has made us what we are, then let us give him the glory for it and tell people what the Lord has done for us.

We *must* do this in order to consolidate and complete the healing experience of our initial encounter with Christ. Sharing our Christian convictions with other people has therapeutic value if only because it compels us to sort out and crystallize those convictions in our own minds. By helping others to understand, we ourselves come to a deeper understanding of what has happened to us. Because we have to be honest with others, therefore we shall be honest with ourselves. We shall not pretend to be what we are not. Moreover, we shall have taken a stand, declared our position and set up standards by which we shall know ourselves judged. Just as the reformed alcoholic loses no opportunity to tell people that he is a reformed alcoholic, so the Christian loses no opportunity to tell people what Christ has done for him. He tells them not only for their sake but for his own sake, knowing that each confession of faith, each act of witness strengthens his commitment and increases the power of Christ within him.

The American Quaker philosopher, Elton Trueblood, writes compellingly about this truth in his excellent book, *The Company of the Committed.** He shows us the therapy of witness in a young forger sentenced for his third term to San Quentin prison in California. This man also was demon-possessed. He hated himself and projected his hatred on everyone, the warders, the world outside and even his fellow-convicts. Then twelve other prisoners, who had formed themselves into a Christian fellowship, invited him to join them.

* Harper and Brothers, New York, 1961.

He did so, suspiciously at first, but discovered to his amazement that they were actually concerned about him. He found that with them he could share his feelings of self-loathing and his hatred for the lucky people who lived outside the prison gate. Within their fellowship the young forger encountered Christ. He learned to study the Bible regularly and to pray by name for the other members of the group. This was, in a sense, the initial shock treatment that drove the demons out of his soul; but he himself completed the cure. He extended his new life, as far as he could, to the entire prison population. He prayed for all his fellow-prisoners, tried to help them and told them how much the Lord had done for him. He followed the therapy of witness. Prison walls still surrounded him, but he became a new and truly liberated person. His healing was complete.

CHAPTER V

WITH A DIVORCEE

IF it can be said that a man reveals his character in his encounters with women, then the Gospels throw a floodlight on the character of Jesus. He encountered a number of women during his earthly ministry, and his conduct towards them appears all the more remarkable when you remember the inferior status of woman in the first-century world. The hard Roman treated her as a slave or a plaything. The cultured Greek did not regard her as the intellectual equal of any man. Even the devout Jew listed her as an item of property along with his fields and cattle and would never break the law by talking to her about religion. The coming of Jesus invested womanhood with a new honour, and motherhood with infinite sacredness. Towards women of all races and ranks, even fallen women, Jesus displayed a gallant courtesy, a knightly chivalry for which he has been well named "the greatest Gentleman of the ages".

This is how we see Jesus in a crucial encounter recorded in the fourth chapter of John's Gospel. Travelling northwards, he and the disciples had to pass through Samaria, the home of their traditional enemies. At midday they stopped to rest near the city of Sychar under the shadow of Mount Gerazim, the very mountain where even today the three hundred surviving Samaritans observe their own Passover every April 15th. Seated by Jacob's Well, while the others went into the city to buy food, Jesus noticed a woman bearing a water jug on her head. He must have thought it strange that she came by herself at noon instead of the usual hour, morning or evening, in company with other women. Was she some sort of social outcast—a prostitute perhaps? Any other Jewish man would have walked away from the well, and no doubt the Samaritan woman showed some surprise when Jesus not only remained but greeted her and engaged her in conversation.

Knowing what we do about this woman, we can hardly identify ourselves with her. Yet there is something very familiar about her encounter with Jesus, a sequence of dialogue, perhaps, which so carries us along that we feel ourselves irresistibly involved in it.

See how graciously Jesus takes the initiative. "Give me a drink," he asks, at once putting himself in her debt. Having journeyed through that hot, dry country and having quenched my thirst at Jacob's Well, I can appreciate how eagerly Jesus longed to taste that clear, cool water. The woman reacted with natural astonishment, "How is it that you, a Jew, ask a drink of me, a woman of Samaria?" Then, observing the embarrassment in her eyes, the lines of cynicism on her face, Jesus said gently, "If you knew the gift of God, and who it is that is saying to you, 'Give me a drink,' you would have asked him, and he would have given you living water." Was this stranger having sport with her? Very well, two could play at that game. "Sir," she retorted sharply, "you have nothing to draw with, and the well is deep; where do you get that living water? . . ." Ignoring her sarcasm, Jesus explained patiently, "Everyone who drinks of this water will thirst again, but whoever drinks of the water that I shall give him will never thirst; the water that I shall give him will become in him a spring of water welling up to eternal life."

Such a gracious approach and so typical of the Master's winsome appeal. He made demands of people but first he offered them a priceless gift. On the very threshold of his ministry, as he wrestled with his soul in the wilderness of temptation, he resolved that this must be the manner of his approach to men. By saying "No" to the tempter Jesus rejected all ignoble means of stampeding men into faith. He would not bully them into believing by rubbing their noses in the dirt of gullibility or helplessness. He would deal with them gently and patiently and would appeal to a longing already in the human heart. Only to such an appeal would people respond.

The woman of Samaria did respond to Jesus. "Sir, give me this water, that I may not thirst nor come here to draw." We cannot believe that she spoke flippantly, as though to say, "If you know a built-in way of quenching thirst, by all means show it to me. Then I shall be spared the trouble of making this tiresome journey to the well every day." It was more likely that at this point Jesus began to establish a spiritual rapport with the woman. She caught the first glimmerings of the truth, and something within her came out to meet it, the confession of a parched soul and the thirst for a cleaner, purer life than she had ever known. In her jaded face Jesus could read the unspoken words, "I am tired of my life, tired of men, tired of adultery, tired of being a social outcast. I pretend to be satisfied, but deep down I know that this is no more than a living death. Where is the real life that you offer me?"

I have met the woman of Samaria, or someone very much like her. Once divorced and twice widowed, she now holds a highly-paid position, lives in an expensive flat, plasters herself with cosmetics, manages to look ten years younger than her age and loses herself in a gay, social whirl. Outwardly she appears happy, but on closer examination you can see lines of cynicism on her hard face, masking the agony of deep discontent. Her voice has a hollow ring. She rarely smiles. She cannot sleep peacefully even with the help of drugs. She has squeezed the world dry of its pleasures, but none satisfy her. She feels that she has lived through everything except life. Though not a religious woman, her soul fairly shrieks the religious question, the longing of many human hearts, "Give me this water, that I may not thirst, nor come here to draw."

To the Samaritan woman Jesus then spoke one rapier-like word that pierced her pretence and bared the sickness of her soul. "Go, call your husband, and come here." Her eyes downcast, the woman said, "I have no husband." With more sorrow than scorn Jesus replied, "You are right in saying, 'I have no husband'; for you have had five husbands, and he whom you now have is not your husband." *That* was a colourful record of legalized adultery. Even our more glamorous film stars have not equalled it; though give them time; some of them are still young. Someone wrote an imaginative novel about this woman's life in which he portrayed her, not as a hardened adulteress but as the victim of a series of unfortunate circumstances. Whatever her background, it was plain that she harboured within her soul an unsolved problem that must be exposed and dealt with before ever she could taste of the living water that Jesus graciously offered.

A distinguished psychiatrist once told me that if he had the time he would like to publish a depth study of the personal ministry of Jesus. He spoke of Jesus as the original psychiatrist, as one whose searching mind quickly probed his patient's personality, whose diagnosis was uncannily accurate and who invariably prescribed the only possible cure. Sometimes even the most skilful analyst has to treat a patient for two years before uncovering the source of his nervous symptoms, but Jesus had to converse with the Samaritan woman for only two minutes before asking her the leading question. "Go and call your husband and come here." This was her real problem, the source of her cynicism and discontent. She needed to face the truth about herself and to admit that she had made a mess of things because of her own undisciplined life. Jesus compelled her to do exactly that. He lifted the lid off her personality, forced her to look down at the sickening sight of her moral weakness and to smell the stench of her uncontrollable lustful nature.

Jesus was always doing that to people. We think of him as the gentle, winsome Man of Galilee whom the common people heard gladly because he brought them comfort and encouragement. Wherever he passed sorrows were healed and diseases cured, shadows lifted from strained minds, and souls restored to health and strength and cleanness. It is a true picture, but study his encounters with people and you will see that often they had to suffer excruciating spiritual agony as a requisite to healing. Like an expert analyst Jesus lifted the lid off their personalities and showed them the rotting refuse of their pride, their prejudice, their greed, their cowardice, their hypocrisies, all the moral weaknesses that they had locked in the vault of their subconscious minds. Graciously he proffered them the gift of life that found a ready response in their hearts, but when they reached out to receive this gift he then forced them to face the truth about themselves.

It still happens. What the historic Jesus did to men and women in ancient Palestine, so the living Christ does to us now in London, Birmingham, New York, or wherever we happen to encounter him. The Gospel story is our story. *You* are the Samaritan woman, *I* am Judas, *this man* is Peter, *that girl* is Mary Magdalene; and whatever Christ does for the healing of our bodies and souls he will do by compelling us to face everything about ourselves which we have not had the courage to face. There is no other way. We may fool ourselves most of the time, we may fool other people some of the time but we cannot fool Christ at all. He knows everything about us, the worst as well as the best; and the moment we encounter him, his pure personality plays on our soul like a searchlight, showing up every ugliness, every blemish, compelling us to absolute self-honesty.

That is why his own contemporaries tried to smash the blinding searchlight into a thousand pieces. Self-honesty involves a terrific strain for any of us. It can be such a forbidding experience, so utterly painful and devastating that we break everything in sight before submitting to so terrible an indignity. The Samaritan woman tried to evade it by raising the conversation to a "spiritual" level. She resorted to the old and safe expedient of discussing the formalities of religion. "Sir, I perceive that you are a prophet. Our fathers worshipped on this mountain; and you say that Jerusalem is the place where men ought to worship." Religion as a means of escape from Christ—it is not unusual even today. As the poet, Francis Thompson, fled from the Hound of Heaven down the labyrinthine ways of his own soul, so we flee from him down the labyrinthine ways of theological controversy, religious ceremonial, ecclesiastical politics and Christian activism. Anything to avoid a solitary, face-to-face confrontation with Christ himself.

Let us ask where the difficulty lies. Why do people avoid an encounter with the Christ who compels them to look honestly at themselves? Inner despair, perhaps—the fear that if they look long and hard enough they will find something wrong, something hopeless and irremediable. A man feels ill and suspects that his recurring symptoms indicate some deep-seated malady which might necessitate drastic and costly treatment; so he doctors himself with patent medicines and home remedies and tries to go about his daily routine as if everything were normal. The one thing he will not do is consult a physician, because he knows that a medical man will diagnose the trouble, lay bare the disease and force him to face the truth about himself. Matthew Arnold said of Goethe that he could lay his finger with unerring accuracy on the real seat of human misery and say, "Thou ailest here and here." Christ does that with men. He strips off the mask of our pretence and sophistication and shows us the sickness of our own souls. That is why some people do not want to encounter him.

Another reason is the fear of inconvenience. People hesitate to look inside themselves because they know that what they see may nauseate them and they have no desire to clean out the mess. An attractive, middle-aged woman sat in my vestry. She had come to talk about her teen-age daughter, a keen member of our Church Youth Club, who had become too seriously involved with a boy many years older than herself. "You are at fault," I told this woman. "The girl has no father. You have been twice divorced. All day long you are out at work, which is hard enough on the girl, but you are out most evenings, too, having a gay time. You give her almost nothing of yourself. Who can blame her if she reaches out elsewhere for affection and security? Forget your daughter for a moment and take a good look at yourself. She is not the delinquent one; you are!" That was more than the indignant mother could take. She had not come to be insulted so she flounced out of my vestry, just as men and women have always flounced out of the presence of Christ.

Another reason for keeping clear of Christ is the fear of fellowship. If that seems strange, look at a human parallel. If a friend in a moment of desperation confides to you something humiliating about himself, you had better expect that soon afterwards he may show resentment towards you. No matter how sympathetically you listen and no matter how gently you deal with him, he is likely to feel that you are secretly laughing at him or have contempt for him. The next morning he will regret having told you so much. He will be angry, because you, whom he has hitherto deceived, now know the truth about him; but angrier still because, having shared his secret with another person, he now has to admit it to himself in a way that he has never done before. Patients tell me that after months of intensive psychoanalysis they begin to develop a dependence upon their doctor and at the same time an antagonism towards him, regretting that they ever came to him in the first place, resenting that they have told him so much and wishing that they had let sleeping dogs lie. That is often a figure of our antagonism towards Christ.

Yet *can* we avoid this crucial encounter with the Great Physician, any more than a sick man can avoid an encounter with a surgeon or psychiatrist, if we really want health of body, mind and spirit? I remember pleading with a stubborn farmer to undergo an essential operation. A physical disability gave him constant pain, impeded his work and even threatened his life. That was serious, because he had nine mouths to feed; and with him removed from the scene, his

wife and children would be destitute. In those days it cost
the earth to be ill, and the poor farmer simply pleaded that
he could not afford the price of an operation. Even when his
kindly neighbours offered to underwrite the medical expenses
and a generous surgeon agreed to charge no fee, this man
still made excuses. The truth was that he had always lived in
the backwoods, had never seen the inside of a hospital and
frankly feared the painful ordeal. Finally he collapsed and
had to be carried to hospital. He suffered all the post-operative
agony, all the misery of convalescence, but once having re-
covered his health he admitted, almost boastfully, "I should
have had it done years ago. I just didn't realize how sick I
was. I feel like a new man now, almost as though I had been
born all over again."

The crucial encounter with Christ need not be altogether
an experience of unrelieved anguish. The thought of it may
terrify us at first, and the encounter itself may be a painful
ordeal, but it will be the pain of an old life dying and a new
life struggling to be born. To people such as we are the Gospel
of Christ opens up a way whereby facing the truth about ourselves can be the most healing, cleansing, comforting experience we have ever known. Because God dwelt in Jesus,
and because the Incarnation means that God has come where
we are and has exposed himself to all the winds of evil that
beat upon the human soul, therefore we shall not be afraid to
face God and to see ourselves through his pure eyes. What we
see may shock us but it will not shock God, because he
knows and understands and loves us in spite of what we are
or may have been. As a condition of the new life that he offers
us, the God who revealed himself in Christ asks only one
thing—that we look inside ourselves and face the truth about
ourselves. When we achieve that condition of inner honesty,
painful as it may be, we shall realize how ill we have been,
because in our new health we shall feel like new creatures
who have been born all over again.

So it happened to the Samaritan woman. Quickly Jesus

pulled her down from the heights of lofty liturgical discussion, saying, in effect, "If you want to talk about worship, we shall do so, but remember this: God is a spirit, and those who worship him must worship him in spirit and in truth. The place and techniques of worship do not matter. What does matter is the sincerity of your worship, the reality of your communion with God. More than all your words, your prayers and your praises, God wants your life, and you had better ask yourself whether the life you are now living will be acceptable to him." Her defences crumbling, the Samaritan woman tried one last evasion—that of postponing the issue, the old expedient which in our idiom says, "Yes, some day I shall have to face God, some day put my life in order, but not now"; the old prayer, "God make me pure, but not yet." She actually said, "I know that Messiah is coming (he who is called Christ); when he comes, he will show us all things." But the issue cannot be postponed. Now is the day of salvation. When Christ encounters us and proffers eternal life, we must reach out for it, else the gift of God may not come within our grasp again. To this loose woman from Samaria Jesus disclosed a truth which the best people, the religious people, did not understand and which even his disciples had not yet recognized. She looked, as they looked, for the Messiah. Jesus said to her, "I who speak to you am he."

So this was it—the Divine visitation which to most of us comes only once, the heaven-sent opportunity of exchanging a living death for a soul pulsating with eternal life. Eagerly the woman grasped it. Recognizing that this was indeed the crucial encounter, she did the courageous thing, faced the truth about herself, went through the agony of self-honesty and accepted from Jesus the gift of healing. More courageously still, she turned from the Master's presence and ran into the city, calling out to the very people who had despised and snubbed her, "Come, see a man who told me all that I ever did. Can this be the Christ?" So convinced were the Samaritans of her sincerity that they rushed out to Jacob's

Well, persuaded Jesus to remain two days in their city and after his departure poured out their thanks to this former adulteress for showing them the way to Christ.

Many such encounters took place in the personal ministry of Jesus, and they still take place—men and women receiving from Christ the gift of new life because they looked honestly at themselves through his eyes and became his witnesses and ambassadors to their fellow-men. There was a university student who led a dissolute life, drinking heavily, conducting himself loosely with women and displaying an ambitious spirit which made it clear that whoever blocked his path would be kicked aside. Surprisingly he became a minister of the Gospel, though how he ever squared his ordination vows with the cesspool of iniquity in his soul remained a mystery to those who knew him. When I met him years later his appearance had so changed that I scarcely recognized him. He looked softened and subdued, like a man who has fought a terrific battle and lost and in defeat has found peace of mind and serenity of soul. He was now the minister of a struggling rural church, doing his work with completely selfless dedication. I asked him no question, and he gave me no answer, but these are the words that I read in his eyes, "Christ has healed me!" Christ can do as much for you.

CHAPTER VI

WITH A FRUSTRATED INVALID

In ancient Jerusalem there was a famous pool—you can see the excavations of it today—known as the Pool of Bethesda, surrounded by five porches. These porches, or cloisters, resembled the out-patients' department of a slum hospital. Jammed into them, thick as flies, was a depressing assortment of sick people, blind, lame and hopeless. They came there for a reason. The pool had medicinal qualities. At intervals it bubbled, as though stirred by an angel hand, and whenever the disturbance took place the invalids surged forward to bathe themselves in its healing waters.

In the fifth chapter of John's Gospel we read about a crippled man who had remained by that pool for thirty-eight years, hoping against hope to be miraculously cured by the healing springs; but each time the water bubbled it was the same story. A horde of screaming invalids swarmed past him, some not half so seriously ill as he, others having waited not half as long, but each fighting for himself, and none stopping to assist this pitiable creature held back by his own infirmity.

One day Jesus came to the Pool of Bethesda and made his way among these human wrecks. His gaze fastened upon the invalid who had laid there paralysed for thirty-eight years, and with tender compassion he asked, "Do you want to be healed?" "Sir," the sick man retorted bitterly, "I have no man to put me into the pool when the water is troubled, and while I am going another steps down before me."

There are physical wrecks who can almost literally identify themselves with this first-century invalid. You will find them in any hospital for incurables. I used to visit two of them in the hope of giving their souls some of the strength denied to their bodies but always I came away suspecting that their souls were stronger than mine. There was Willie who at the age of thirty-eight fell from a barn roof and fractured his spine. For twenty years he had lain under the sheets like a human log covered in white, totally paralysed except for his eyes. Willie talked with his eyes and he smiled with them. There was Mr. Sands, an arthritic cripple, whose limbs were all twisted and curled like the roots of a tree. He enjoyed watching western films on television, because the scenery of mountains and trees and broad fields transported him to the outside world which he had not seen for three decades.

The frustrated man by the Pool of Bethesda represents a much larger company than one finds in a hospital for incurables. "Sir, I have no man to put me into the pool when the water is troubled, and while I am going another steps down before me." You need not be an invalid to utter that cry which echoes the complaint of a multitude of human hearts. Many people feel that they have been frustrated. They believe that God endowed them with all the normal abilities and ambitions which, given the opportunity to develop, might really have amounted to something; but all their lives something has held them back—poor health, the lack of a formal education, a bad marriage or no marriage, crushing family responsibilities or sheer circumstances. Now they have become cynics, crying out bitterly, "I never had a chance," or they may simply have lapsed into sad resignation, nursing a grudge against life because it treated them unfairly and passed them by.

On a never-to-be-forgotten day a new factor entered the lame beggar's situation. He encountered Christ, the Great Physician of our bodies and souls. Christ cured him, but not until he had asked a question which at first seems pointless, callous and almost cruel—"Do you want to be healed?" We have no record of his reply, but we can readily imagine it: "Want to be healed? Why do you think I've been hanging about this stinking out-patients' department—I, shut into a horrible, living death, I, who know nothing about real life in its strength and fulness? Every day for thirty-eight years I have struggled towards that pool, 14,000 times in all, every time hoping for a cure and every time pushed back. And you ask me if I want to be healed!"

But is it such a pointless question? We must consider the possibility, as Jesus no doubt considered it, that this poor cripple did not, in fact, want to be healed. I am quite certain that Mr. Sands does not want to be healed. He knows only too well that after thirty years of confinement he could never rehabilitate himself in the outside world. He is satisfied to view that world through a television screen. The hospital ward has become his home, and despite his disability, he is quite happy and content. In his heart the first-century invalid might also have been content with idleness under the cool porches of Bethesda, while hale and hearty men toiled and perspired under the burden and heat of the day. So long as he remained there, an impoverished cripple, his neighbours would pity him and minister to his wants; but the moment he emerged from those healing waters in the full vigour of health he would cease to be an object of charity and would have to look out for himself. Consider it possible, therefore, that while he appeared to make the effort and complained of being held back by outside forces, yet day after day a more powerful inner force held him back and deterred him from actually entering the pool.

Our Lord's question was typical of the intensely *personal* nature of his ministry to individuals. To him a cripple was not a cripple but a man with human needs that went far deeper than the surface sickness visible to ordinary eyes. In asking this frustrated invalid, "Do you want to be healed?" Jesus brought some of those needs out into the open and compelled the man, as he compelled other people, to face the truth about himself.

This is always a feature of our crucial encounter with

Christ. Before his healing power can touch our situation we must subject ourselves to an exercise of self-honesty. Of everyone who feels plagued by a sense of unfulfilment the living Christ asks some very frank questions and expects us to come up with some equally frank answers. "Do you want to be healed?" he asks. "Do you really desire the things in life which you claim to have been denied? Have you got what it takes to qualify for those dreams and ambitions which you say have been thwarted by circumstances beyond your control? If your coveted goals were brought within reach, would you pay the price to grasp them and hang on to them?"

If we pondered these questions many of us would be forced in all honesty to answer "No!" We do not want to be healed, we have not got what it takes and we are not willing to pay the price. Sometimes in the school of life we have to learn that lesson the hard way. I knew a very fine soprano who for years fancied herself as a potential prima donna. It drove her mad to attend a performance or listen to other singers on the radio. Always she exclaimed bitterly, "I have a better voice than any of them but I have just never had any of the breaks. Ability means nothing in this profession. It's not what you know but who you know that counts. If only I could once get an audition!" She did manage to get an audition with the Metropolitan Opera Company in New York. It took place in a studio in Rockefeller Center where she found herself in faster company than she could ever have imagined—the company of artists younger, more attractive, more gifted, more dedicated and certainly more determined than herself. A pair of imposing maestros listened to her and said tonelessly, "Don't call us; we'll call you." That ended her dreams about becoming a prima donna. After that she sang for the joy of it, faced up to the truth about herself and buried her sense of frustration for ever.

Perhaps Jesus had a more important reason for asking the lame beggar, "Do you want to be healed?" At the root of his frustration there may have been a spiritual problem which must be exposed and dealt with before he could be made completely well, a problem which had been growing with the years—the feeling of resentment towards other people. We can understand it easily enough. Whenever the waters began to swirl and bubble he nearly made it; but each time other invalids who were not so infirm as he, who had friends to assist them, pressed forward, brushing him aside or climbing over him, leaving him behind in the feverish scramble. How he must have cursed this "every-man-for-himself" rat race! You can well imagine that the troubled waters of the pool seemed placid compared to the seething cauldron of hatred that boiled in the poor invalid's heart and aggravated his physical infirmity. What bitter resentment he must have felt towards his companions in misery who stepped into the healing waters and came forth cured and restored!

"Sir, I have no man to put me into the pool when the water is troubled, and while I am going, *another steps down before me.*" Is that not often the source of frustration? Is it not often the burden of our own complaint—that we have been held back, not through any fault of our own, but because other people, more cunning and aggressive than we are, have pushed themselves ahead of us and blocked our path? Psychologists call this complaint in its more acute form a "persecution complex", and when it becomes distressingly acute, only a qualified psychologist can deal with it. You recognize it immediately in a patient. He has the "poor little me" attitude. He sees the entire human race as a conspiracy ganged up against him and he speaks of the forces that hold him back as "they", though he can never quite define who "they" really are. It gives point to the question of a character in a play by Jean-Paul Sartre, "What is hell?", and the cynical answer, "Hell? That is other people."

Most of us, however, could deal constructively with our sense of frustration if we were to read, mark, learn and inwardly digest Emerson's essay on "Compensation". Emerson sees in the whole economy of nature a levelling-off process, an unwritten law of compensation which, if it deprives a man of one advantage rewards him with another, and which, if it gives him one blessing takes another away. "For everything you have missed," writes Emerson, "you have gained something else, and for everything you gain you lose something." Let us once realize that, and we shall not curse our own deprivations nor shall we envy the man who seems to have prospered, because if we look at him more closely we shall discover that he also has his deprivations and that in some respects he is less favoured than we are.

Thornton Wilder explored the truth of compensation in his brief play, *The Angel that Troubled the Waters*. As the frustrated invalid by the Pool of Bethesda prayed that God would touch his tortured body into health, an angel whispered in his ear, "Stand back; healing is not for you. Without your wound where would your power be? It is your very remorse that makes your low voice tremble in the hearts of men. Not the angels themselves in heaven can persuade the wretched and blundering children of earth as can one human being broken on the wheels of living. In love's service only the wounded soldiers can serve." Then the angel stepped into the waters and troubled them. As the lone sufferer drew back, a lame old neighbour, smiling his thanks, made his painful way into the pool and was healed. Joyously, with a song on his lips, he approached the other, still standing like a statue of grief. "Perhaps," he said, "it will be your turn next. But meanwhile come with me to my house. My son is lost in dark thoughts. I do not understand him. Only you have ever lifted his moods. And my daughter, since her child has died, sits in the shadow. She will not listen to us. Only you can help her. Come with me but an hour."

That could have been his compensation—a health of mind and soul denied to the physically sound; and he only jeopardized that health by nursing within himself the cancer of envy and resentment. Do we feel that life has unfairly held us back? Do we blame other people for this and bear a grudge against them because they seem to have forged ahead and grasped our coveted opportunities? Let us look more closely at the facts of their lives, at the price they have paid for their success, their sense of unfulfilment because they lack some of the blessings that we take for granted, and we shall not be so eager to exchange places with them. When our envy gives way to sympathy and our resentment to love, we shall have gone far towards uprooting the source of our own frustration. "The mountainous inequalities vanish," writes Emerson. "Love reduces them as the sun melts the iceberg in the sea. The heart and soul of all men being one, this bitterness of *His* and *Mine* ceases . . . He is mine. I am my brother and my brother is me."

"Do you want to be healed?" That question which Jesus asked the frustrated invalid has implications for all of us who feel thwarted by a sense of unfulfilment. Having answered it honestly, we can turn from the stage of conjecture to the audience of real life. Satisfied that the man did want to be healed, Christ cured him. He cured him not by assisting him into the pool, not by fulfilling an ambition which had been denied for thirty-eight years, but by introducing into his predicament a totally new and unexpected factor which entirely transcended the frustration and cancelled it out of existence. "Rise," he commanded, "take up your pallet and walk." John in his Gospel concludes this part of the story by saying, "And at once the man was healed, and he took up his pallet and walked."

Of the Holy Communion, Thomas à Kempis wrote that if the sacrament "were to be celebrated in one place only, and consecrated by only one priest in the world", how irresistibly we should be attracted to that place and that priest. We may say also that even if the Great Physician had performed no other mighty work than that of healing the lame beggar, his power would attract us like a magnet. We know, however, that this crucial encounter by the Pool of Bethesda was only one pearl in a string of miracles that stretches throughout his entire personal ministry. Whenever Jesus entered a human situation, however hopeless, he brought into it a new, transforming factor that changed sickness to health, weakness to strength, sorrow to joy, defeat into victory.

The living Christ continues his healing ministry. Still he comes to frustrated men and women and, though he may not remove all the impediments and obstacles that hold us back, yet by his grace and power he does redeem us from the feeling of frustration. When Christ encounters us he introduces into our lives totally new and unexpected factors that change our essential situation. He does it in one of three ways—by opening a new door to God's purpose, by helping us to live creatively within our limitations, or by extending our vision beyond the defeats of time to the triumph of eternity. Only life itself can validate this truth; and for that reason we shall look at the lives of three people.

The late Lloyd C. Douglas, author of many inspiring books, was in his early career a minister of the Gospel. Some thirty-five years ago he became pastor of a church so affluent and ultra-conservative that it broke his spirit, forced his resignation and nearly drove him out of the ministry altogether. For Dr. Douglas that brief pastorate was an agonizing frustration. After enjoying happiness and success in his former congregations he felt as if he were beating his head against a stone wall. He had often toyed with the idea of writing a work of fiction and had even tried his hand at it, but the pressure of pastoral duties deterred him. Now, having reached a dead-end in his career, he began to think of it more seriously. One Sunday, after he had preached a searching sermon about secrecy in good works, his family suggested that it might make a suitable theme for a novel. The idea took fire in his mind, and with a re-awakened sense of purpose Dr. Douglas settled down to write a book called *Magnificent Obsession*, a book that made him famous and opened for him the door to unlimited Christian influence.* Christ did not help this frustrated minister into the pool; rather he removed the necessity of the pool by introducing a new factor into his situation.

By sheer indomitable faith Helen Keller, blind, deaf and dumb from childhood, developed her other senses sufficiently to qualify for entrance to university. Describing her first day at Radcliffe, she tells us that a potent force within her, stronger than the persuasion of her friends, stronger even than the pleadings of her heart, inspired her to try her strength by the standards of those who see and hear. She knew that there were obstacles in her way but she was eager to overcome them. She had taken to heart the words of the wise Roman who wrote, "To be banished from Rome is but to live outside of Rome." Debarred from the great highways of knowledge, she resolved to make the journey by unfrequented paths; and she knew that in college there were many by-paths where she could touch hands with girls who were thinking, loving and struggling like herself.† Christ did not help this supremely frustrated woman into the pool but Christ redeemed Helen Keller from frustration by helping her to live creatively even within the most crippling limitations.

I once knew a woman who spoke proudly of her sister. This was surprising, because for years before her death the sister had been confined to a wheelchair. Yet this woman found it no trial to care for her. "You should have known my sister," she used to say. "You would have admired her as I did. She never complained, never felt sorry for herself, never resented the fact that she was an incurable invalid. She had so much of the grace of Christ within her that it shone through her eyes like a benediction. She brought cheer to everybody.

---

* As told in *The Shape of Sunday*, an Intimate Biography of Lloyd C. Douglas, by Virginia Douglas Dawson and Betty Douglas Wilson (Thomas Allen, Ltd., Toronto, 1952).

† Helen Keller, *The Story of My Life* (Hodder and Stoughton, London, 1959).

Wherever she appeared even the children stopped their play and ran over to talk with her." Through tears of memory this woman told me that one day, as she pushed the wheel-chair along the street, the sense of sorrow overwhelmed her and she cried out to her beloved sister, "How I wish you could run like those children!" The sister turned her smiling face and replied, "Never mind, my dear. When you and I meet in the Kingdom of God the first thing we're going to do is have a race." Christ had not helped this remarkable invalid into the pool but he had given her a hope of Heaven that re-deemed her from all earthly frustration.

CHAPTER VII

WITH A SOCIAL SNOB

ONE of the basic attitudes of which we shall have to be cured, before we can hope to relieve the tensions that keep our world on the edge of catastrophe, is the attitude of sheer snobbery. Deeply rooted in human nature, it sends out prickly plants that injure and choke relationships on every level of social and international life. The racial conflict, which has erupted so viciously and violently in our time, is the poisonous fruit of the white man's self-delegated supremacy over peoples of other skin colours. Communism, in its different degrees, springs from the soil of class-consciousness and flourishes where men have been exploited and treated condescendingly by their supposed social "superiors".

We all have our mental image of a snob depending upon where we have had the misfortune to meet him, whether in an officers' mess, a Senior Common Room, a shop in Mayfair or even in a church. He is the person who, because he happens to possess certain hereditary, social, economic, intellectual or spiritual advantages, looks down his nose on lesser mortals who do not possess those advantages. There is something of the snob in all of us. In the satirical review, *Beyond the Fringe*, the four members of the cast in mock seriousness compliment themselves that their association together has proved to be a wholesome democratic experience, because one character, though sporting a public school tie, is Jewish, while another speaks with the accent of the lower classes. But here is the punch line, "Wouldn't it be awful to be a Jew *and* come from the lower classes?" Every man likes to feel that he can look down on somebody. Every man, no matter what his social status, draws a circle which includes all whom he regards as his equals and excludes a vast company whom he regards as his inferiors and towards whom he has no fellow-feeling.

There used to be a jingle about "Good old Boston, the home of the bean and the cod, where the Lowells speak only to the Cabots and the Cabots speak only to God". I wonder what God that was. It couldn't have been the God who sent his Son to be born in a Bethlehem stable. Some men do draw a very small circle.

Once Jesus encountered such a man. The Master had been preaching to a mixed company about eternal life when suddenly a lawyer stood up and asked with seeming sincerity, "Teacher, what shall I do to inherit eternal life?" Sensing the man's subtle purpose, Jesus replied, "What is written in the law? How do you read?" Like a parrot the lawyer rattled off the rule book, "You shall love the Lord your God with all your heart, and with all your soul, and with all your strength, and with all your mind; and your neighbour as yourself." "You have answered right," Jesus said with a smile, "do this, and you will live." But the lawyer was not to be put off so easily, for then he sprang his trap. "And who," he asked innocently, "is my neighbour?"

The late John Baillie suggests that only a lawyer would ask a simple question like that. He says that anybody else would have found the word "neighbour" clear and plain enough, but lawyers seem to find nothing clear until they have decked it out in long rigmaroles, so that all who are not lawyers will find it ten times more obscure.* However, the question was not so simple as it sounded, because the Jewish law did draw some fairly clear distinctions among people to whom the word "neighbour" applied. Besides, this lawyer had a much baser and shabbier motive. He *wanted* the word "neighbour" to be an obscure word. He wanted, as the Gospel tells us, "to justify

* John Baillie, *A Reasoned Faith* (Oxford University Press, London, 1963), p. 3.

himself". He obviously had his own definite ideas about the classes of people whom he should or should not regard as his neighbours, and these were ideas that others sitting in the audience that day would heartily endorse. Therefore, his seemingly innocent question placed Jesus in a somewhat delicate position.

To get at the crux of this incident we have to go back a few hundred years in Jewish history. In the sixth century before Christ Jerusalem was sacked by the Babylonian army, and the better classes of the Jews carried away to Babylon in exile. Some of the exiles saw the hand of God in their sufferings and grew spiritually in the years of captivity. Others tended to become hard and bitter and intolerant. The whole experience drove iron into their souls and engendered within them an inverted snobbery towards all who were not of their race or religion. Given their freedom, they returned to their own country and found a population mixed by intermarriage with peoples from surrounding nations. This arrangement could have enriched the Jewish community, but the returned exiles regarded it as evil and as a sin in the sight of God. Therefore they made their first act the banishment of all foreigners from the land. They drove them out of their homes, confiscated their property, compelled the Jews to divorce their foreign wives and husbands, and without any humanitarian feeling broke families asunder. The circle of racial and religious exclusiveness had been drawn; and upon all who stood outside that circle the Jews looked down their noses with contempt.

Not all the descendants of Abraham condoned this snobbery. The Old Testament book of *Jonah*, written in the form of a parable, is a hot protest from the pen of some high-minded Jew to warn his people that they have denied the noblest ideals in their heritage and flouted all the humanitarian teachings of the great prophets. Let them see themselves in the unlovely Jonah, the narrow-minded patriot, the religious bigot, the arch-snob whom God rebukes because he

cares more for a garden plant than he does for people who
differ from him. But snobbery dies hard, especially in those
who make it a compensation for their own sense of in-
feriority; and by the time of Jesus the Jews had been so
economically and politically humiliated by one world power
after another that they could only compensate by tightening
the circle and looking disdainfully upon those whom Kipling
called "lesser breeds without the law".

Automatically the circle of neighbourliness excluded all
Gentiles, all non-Jews. Indeed, some of the rabbis declared it
illegal to help a Gentile woman in childbirth, for that would
only have been to bring another Gentile into the world. Particularly it excluded the people of Samaria, those despised
half-breeds who traced their ancestry to the period of intermarriage during the exile. Though they lived next door, the
Samaritans were not to be regarded as neighbours, and any
Jew found treating them as such could expect to suffer the
penalty of the law. So it was not only a real question but a
burning question that the lawyer asked Jesus when he said
innocently, "Who is my neighbour?"

Jesus gave him an answer, an answer so final and definitive
that the question never needs to be asked again. It took the
form of a parable which even after two thousand years cap-
tures the imagination of Christians and non-Christians alike.
I have often wondered what this snobbish lawyer would think
if he came back from the dead and learned that one of the
greatest stories ever told, a story which statesmen in every
age have seen as the only blueprint for world peace, was
originally told for his private benefit. But that was so typical
of the intensely personal character of our Lord's ministry.
Jesus spoke not to situations but to people. Many of his
teachings, which have since achieved the most timeless and
universal application, were directed in the first instance to the
particular needs of an individual. They should be read with
that in mind, simply because we can recognize ourselves in
some of these individuals, even in the snobbish lawyer whose

D

question, "Who is my neighbour?", triggered off the story that we are about to recall.

Every child can recite the opening sentence, "A certain man went down from Jerusalem to Jericho . . ." "Poor devil!" the audience must have muttered. Jerusalem is 2,300 feet above sea level, and Jericho, the lowest spot on earth, is 1,300 feet below sea level; so that in little more than twenty miles your stomach has to drop some 3,600 feet. It is still a nauseating journey despite the improved road surface. In Bible days it was a narrow, tortuous road of sudden turnings and rocky defiles that made it a happy hunting-ground for bandits and brigands. No man travelled that road unless he had to and then he travelled it in peril of his life, knowing that any moment he might be attacked and robbed, beaten and perhaps killed.

So it happened to the man in the story. Thieves pounced on him, worked him over with "coshes", ransacked his belongings and left him lying in the ditch, half-dead. A priest, safeguarded, perhaps, by his religious insignia, passed the scene of the crime, noticed the dying victim but kept right on going. Later a Levite did the same thing. Though the wounded man was a Jew, a fellow-countryman, the Priest and Levite evidently did not regard him as a "neighbour". Now comes the punch line to *this* drama, "But a certain Samaritan . . ." You can see the shocked expression on the lawyer's face. You can hear the snort of disgust that went up from the audience. Posterity calls him the "Good Samaritan", but in the minds of those who heard the story from the lips of Jesus there were no good Samaritans. The only good Samaritan was a dead one. Yet this despised foreigner, of whose kindness we can read in the tenth chapter of Luke's Gospel, represents in terms of real life our Lord's answer to the snobbish lawyer's question, "Who is my neighbour?"

Before examining what that answer was, let us examine what it was not. It was not a theological answer. Jesus did not attempt to cure human snobbery by appealing to the mind.

He could very well have done that, for we do need to be reminded that God has, in fact, created all men equal and that
in God's sight a man is a man, whatever his nationality or the
colour of his skin. "Hath not a Jew eyes? Hath not a Jew
hands, organs, dimensions, senses, affections, passions? Fed
with the same food, hurt with the same weapons, subject to
the same diseases, healed by the same means, warmed and
cooled by the same winter and summer, as a Christian is?
If you prick us, do we not bleed? If you tickle us, do we not
laugh? If you poison us, do we not die?" So argued the
pathetic Shylock. Intellectually his argument is unassailable
but it is also ineffective. Centuries of anti-Semitism culminat-
ing in the most monstrous atrocities ever committed against
the human race prove that the convinced mind alone does not
cure a man of snobbery.

We cannot call our Lord's parable a sentimental answer. He
did not attempt to cure snobbery by appealing to the human
heart. We can be everlastingly grateful that Jesus spared his
audience that day a sermon on brotherhood and love. These
noble clichés lie at the root of so much unlovely hypocrisy.
Some of the greatest preachers of the brotherhood of man
have been notoriously bad brothers inside their own homes.
The social reformer who champions the cause of the underdog is often the last man prepared to share his kennel. People
who write letters about moral love have a habit of dipping
their pens in the ink of vitriolic hatred. Many of us condemn
prejudice only because our prejudices have never been put
to the test. Seated at my dinner-table, a distinguished
American negro preacher said, "You entertain me in your
home and treat me as an equal, but would you feel the same
way if my family moved in next door or if you and I were
candidates for the same vacant pulpit?"

The answer inherent in the parable of the Good Samaritan
was neither theological nor sentimental but pre-eminently
practical. Jesus attempted to cure snobbery by appealing not
to the mind or the emotions but to the will. After contrasting

the callousness of the priest and Levite with the sacrificial concern of the Good Samaritan, he rephrased the question in a way that really mattered: "Which of these three, do you think, proved neighbour to the man who fell among robbers?" Red-faced with embarrassment and knowing that he had been caught out, the lawyer had to answer, "The one who showed mercy on him." "Exactly," Jesus replied in effect; "and," he added, "if you really want to know who your neighbour is, the man whom the law commands you to love as you love yourself, then you go and find somebody and do for him as the Samaritan did."

So the question, "Who is my neighbour?" turns out to be one that every man must answer for himself; and he will answer it not by what he thinks of people or by how he feels towards them but by what he *does* for them. Your neighbour is the person to whom you *prove* yourself neighbourly; and that person may or may not come within the accidental and artificial boundaries of colour, class and culture. Boundaries exist, to be sure, but the point of our Lord's parable, as exemplified by the religious professionals on the one hand and by the Good Samaritan on the other, is that such boundaries have nothing to do with neighbourliness. The human race is not a collection of college fraternities where we must be brotherly to those within our circle and need not be brotherly to those who stand outside. We create our own circle, and it includes precisely those people, whatever their race, colour, creed or social status, to whom we show a fellow-feeling. To realize this and act upon it is the cure for snobbery.

During the war some soldiers in France brought the body of a dead comrade to a French cemetery to have him buried there. The priest told them gently that it was a Roman Catholic cemetery and that he was duty-bound to ask if their friend had been a baptized Catholic. They said that they did not know. The priest replied that he was sorry but in such circumstances he could not permit burial in his churchyard. Sadly the soldiers took their comrade and buried him six feet beyond the fence of the churchyard. Next day they returned to visit the grave but to their utter astonishment they could find no evidence of freshly-dug soil. As they stood there bewildered, the priest came up and told them that early in the morning he had risen from his bed and with his own hands had moved the fence to include the body of the soldier who had died for France.* The rules and regulations put up the fence, but love moved it. That is the cure for snobbery.

Make no mistake. Snobbery does need to be cured because, though it cannot be called a sickness, it is an abnormality of spirit which hurts the snob as much as it hurts the target of his snobbery. A man cannot injure so much as the feelings of a fellow-man without losing something of his own manhood. Jesus came to make men whole. That was his constant question—"Will you be made whole?" If wholeness denotes a perfect blending of all the elements in our physical, mental and spiritual life, then no man can be a balanced, well integrated personality who allows his relationships to be stultified by barriers which he did not create. Such a man carries within himself an unconscious supply of misery and he will never be rid of it until he takes the initiative and breaks down those barriers with hands of loving kindness.

Let us take this lesson to its farthest extreme and apply it to the one group which all men feel justified in excluding from the circle of love—their professed enemies. Jesus singled out the Samaritans, not only because they differed from the Jews racially and ethnically but because the Jews and Samaritans were traditional enemies. Moreover, they were enemies living next door to each other, and that gives teeth to the parable. The idealist preaches piously about our duty to "love" foreign nations but what duty does he acknowledge to the foreign family next door with whom he finds it difficult to get along? It has been suggested that we should come

* As told by William Barclay in The Daily Study Bible, *The Letters to the Galatians and Ephesians* (The Saint Andrew Press, Edinburgh, 1958), p. 135.

closer to the heart of New Testament teaching if we took the command about "loving our enemies" to mean that we ought to love the people near at hand whom we find most temperamentally incompatible with us. When once we have enlarged the circle of kindness to include the very individuals whom we normally dislike, those who have disagreed with us and perhaps injured us, when we have proved ourselves neighbours to *them*, then we can claim to be cured of the last symptoms of snobbery.

In his distinguished book, *Through the Valley of the Kwai*,* Captain Ernest Gordon, now a Christian Minister, describes his internment in a Japanese prison camp during the war. Degraded to the status of animals by the brutality of their captors, the starved, disease-ridden prisoners lived like animals. Every man's hand was against every other's. They hated, they cursed, they stole among themselves, they watched one another die without feelings. Then came a religious awakening in this jungle hell, a movement of the Holy Spirit that effected a miraculous change in these hopeless prisoners of war. They became neighbours, they worked together for the common good, they helped one another to live. Men even sacrificed their lives for their brothers. The great miracle happened when they were being transported to another camp and found themselves on the same track with several carloads of Japanese wounded. These creatures looked even more neglected and pitiable. Ignoring the threats of the guards, some of the British prisoners went over to them, gave them water and food and began dressing their wounds. "What bloody fools you are!" shouted an Allied officer from another section of the train. Captain Gordon turned to him. "Have you never heard the story of the man who was going from Jerusalem to Jericho?" he asked. The officer looked at him blankly, so Captain Gordon told him the parable of the Good Samaritan in modern and rather earthy language. "But that's different!" the officer protested angrily. "That's in the Bible.

* Harper and Row, New York and Evanston 1962.

These are the swine who have starved us and beaten us. These are our enemies!" "My enemy is my neighbour," came the reply.

Captain Gordon suddenly realized that there was a time when those words would have sounded as ridiculous to him as they did to the disgusted officer. Once he and his fellow-prisoners had nothing but hate in their hearts and never would they have lifted a hand to help a wounded enemy. For eighteen months, however, they had been growing not only in love but in their companionship with the One who was love incarnate. Unforgettable in itself, valuable as a rule of life, the story of the Good Samaritan has authority because Jesus told it and because it is, in fact, a self-portrait of Jesus. His circle of love knew no boundaries; it included every race, every class, every creed; and when his enemies nailed him to a cross, he enlarged the circle and took them in also, praying to God, "Father, forgive them, for they know not what they do."

No, snobbery is not a sickness; it is a sin, and from sin we need to be saved. That is the only cure for snobbery—not simply to follow Christ's teachings but to follow Christ himself, to believe in him and live with him, until his spirit becomes our spirit, his kindness our kindness, and we can exclude no man from the circle of love, because we shall see all our fellow-men through the loving eyes of Christ.

CHAPTER VIII

WITH A PETTY PERFECTIONIST

NOTICE how often the Gospel story sets two personalities in contrast with each other, the one attractive and the other not so attractive—the Prodigal Son against the background of his elder brother; the beggar, Lazarus against Dives, the rich man; the Publican against the Pharisee praying in the temple, and the Dying Thief against his unrepentant associate. Reading the tenth chapter of *Luke*, we see this contrast in the familiar incident of Mary and Martha, Mary definitely emerging as the favourite, especially in the light of our Lord's gentle rebuke to her sister: *"Martha, Martha, thou art careful and troubled about many things: but one thing is needful, and Mary hath chosen that good part, which shall not be taken away from her."*

Yet we feel a sneaking sympathy for Martha because we can so easily visualize the situation. All morning there had been a bustle of excitement in the Bethany home. Jesus was coming for dinner. Jesus, the great Teacher and Worker of miracles, who had recalled even their own brother from the dead, was about to honour this ordinary house with his presence at a meal.

There would be much work to be done in preparation for so distinguished a guest. Perhaps, as is often the case, the main burden of responsibility fell on the willing shoulders of one member of the family. Since daybreak Martha had swept and scrubbed and dusted, darting in and out of the kitchen, almost frantically preparing the food and putting the place in order for this important occasion. Meanwhile Mary had been conspicuously invisible, arranging her clothes and grooming herself to receive the honoured visitor.

Then Jesus arrived. Immediately Mary took charge of him, assuming the role of hostess, engaging in brilliant conversation, sitting at his feet and drinking in his heavenly words. Martha, on the other hand, continued her slaving, turning over the meat, cutting up the fruits and vegetables and doing the hundred and one things which in her efficient mind needed to be done. You can just imagine her mounting indignation. What was Mary thinking about, leaving all the skivvy work to her? Surely Jesus could see the injustice of the situation!

At length, unable to contain herself any longer, she burst out of the kitchen and cried, "Lord, do you not care that my sister has left me to serve alone?" Yes, we can sympathize with Martha; and in the light of her predicament the Master's rebuke does seem a bit unfair. Rudyard Kipling shared our sympathy when he wrote poetically:

> The Sons of Mary seldom bother, for they have inherited
>   that good part,
> But the Sons of Martha favour their mother of the careful
>   soul and the troubled heart;
> And because she lost her temper once, and because she was
>   rude to the Lord, her guest,
> Her Sons must wait upon Mary's Sons—world without
>   end, reprieve or rest.
>
> It is their care in all the ages to take the buffet and cushion
>   the shock,
> It is their care that the gear engages; it is their care that the
>   switches lock:
> It is their care that the wheels run truly; it is their care to
>   embark and entrain,
> Tally, transport and deliver duly the Sons of Mary by land
>   and by main.

*And the Sons of Mary smile and are blessed—they know
　the angels are on their side,
They know in them is the grace confessed, and for them
　are the mercies multiplied.
They sit at the Feet—they hear the Word—they know how
　truly the Promise runs.
They have cast their burden upon the Lord, and—the Lord
　he lays it on Martha's Sons.*

It is a good thing that our society has its Marthas who are
willing to roll up their sleeves and get on with the menial,
thankless tasks while the Marys indulge in their day-dreaming.
The Marthas keep the wheels of life turning. We can describe
them as the efficient people, those with a capacity for detail
who notice the little things that need to be done and do not
consider themselves above doing them. Every good wife and
mother must have something of Martha in her, else her husband's meals will not be cooked nor her children's socks
mended, and soon the household machinery will grind to a
standstill. If you hear a business executive boast of his secretary as a "treasure", you may be sure that he values her
ability to anticipate and handle the details, leaving him free
for his larger responsibilities. The average local congregation
would quickly go defunct if its membership were composed
only of spiritually-minded Marys; it needs a few practical-
minded Marthas to work in the kitchen and inspect the
property and administer finances and do all the purely
mechanical things essential to its existence as a Christian
community.

Yet Jesus rebuked Martha; he spoke words that compared
her unfavourably with her less practical sister. Why? Not for
a moment may we suppose that he was critical of her
efficiency or that he failed to appreciate her solicitude for his
material comfort. His concern was for Martha herself. He
saw that she not only had a capacity for life's details but that

she had allowed herself to become enslaved to them. Details distracted her. She worried about them and let them get her down. The *Revised Standard Version* translates his rebuke, "Martha, you are anxious and troubled about many things," and the *New English Bible* puts it, "You are fretting and fussing."

When we study the personal ministry of Jesus to individuals we see that often the Master compelled people to face a very important truth about themselves. He did this to Martha. With a single statement he diagnosed her besetting weakness— not efficiency but over-efficiency, not a capacity for details but an enslavement to details. Martha was a petty perfectionist. She so busied herself with the little things of life that she neglected the big things, "that good part" as Jesus called them. In college terminology Martha was "majoring on minors".

"Anxious and troubled about many things"—those words may speak to one of our besetting problems. Suppose we take stock of our lives, of the concerns that dominate our thoughts, the matters we most worry about, the things that get us down and break our morale. Are they not often the little things, the petty, materialistic details of life—the dinner menu, the arrangement of furniture, the broken ornament, the scratch on the car door, the stale bread that the baker left yesterday. We do fret and fuss about these things, and if this be the case, we also need to be rebuked. We also need to be brought up sharply to face the truth about ourselves, lest enslavement to detail should do to us what it did to Martha.

Certainly it tended to make her unhappy in herself. Can you not just picture Martha's appearance as she came bursting through the kitchen door, her face flushed, her hair untidy, and a look of strained anxiety in her eyes? Rarely does the efficient person give the appearance of being happy. He tends to perform his duties with a kind of martyred resignation, heaving great virtuous sighs, as though nothing would ever be done unless he did it, but obviously deriving no enjoyment from his efficiency.

It is not surprising that Jesus addressed this particular rebuke to a woman, a housekeeper, because she of all people is susceptible to the dis-ease of "administrivia". "I do wish mother were not such a slave to the house and the family," said one girl. "She has no outside interests and she won't let any of us help her. 'It's my duty,' she keeps saying; but it makes her so tired and irritable." You find the same attitude in the conscientious secretary who remains glued to her office desk after everyone has left for the day. No use telling her to go home. She chooses to make a martyr of herself. "Someone has to take care of these things," she complains, rummaging about in the filing cabinet, but you can see that she doesn't enjoy it one bit. A novelist makes one of his characters say, "Ah, the little troubles, they ruin a woman's life"; and perhaps that is why we apply the term "old woman" to a man who makes himself miserable by a constant haggling over trivialities.

Martha's efficiency not only made her unhappy in herself; it made other people unhappy too. Her petulant outburst in the presence of Jesus, her downright rudeness to her own sister, would certainly inject an unpleasant tension into an otherwise pleasant atmosphere. The trouble with efficient people is that they expect everyone else to be efficient and they have a way of making the rest of us feel guilty if we fail to share their concern for life's details. Have you never been tempted to explode at some over-busy Martha, "Oh, sit down for a few minutes! You make me tired just to look at you!"?

We pay a price if we allow our pettiness to make other people miserable. A business executive entertained some clients at an expensive restaurant. Twice he commanded the waitress to return his steak to the kitchen, first because it was too bloody and then because it was too well done. By this time he had reduced the poor girl to tears and his clients to embarrassment and by his pettiness had spoiled a good dinner and, perhaps, a good contract. The cause of many broken marriages can be traced not to any major incompatibility but to the build-up of little tensions. The husband, if his meals were not served precisely on time, punished his wife by a stern silence; the wife, if her husband forgot to hang up his clothes or left cigarette butts lying around the house, punished him with unbeautiful nagging. Grounds for divorce? Enslavement to life's details!

More seriously still, Martha's capacity for detail had distorted her whole perspective and caused her to lose sight of the really important things. In this case the important thing was the visit of Jesus to her home. Her friendship and that of Mary and their brother meant a great deal to Jesus. "See how he loved him," the Jews said, when they saw Jesus weeping by the tomb of Lazarus. Therefore, it needed someone to remind Martha that Jesus had not come to eat her food; he had come to spend a quiet day with her and her family. A charming hostess can open a tin of baked beans for her guests so long as she remains a charming hostess, but the most lavish banquet will not compensate for her failure to create a welcome and congenial atmosphere.

It is perilous to allow the mechanics of life to interfere with living. Very soon after my ordination I realized how subtly the Church succumbs to the disease of "administrivia", and that, if he is not careful, a minister may so busy himself with the mere mechanics of running a church that he leaves no time for the salvation of souls and loses sight of the main purpose of his ministry. It is said that the secret of John Wesley's power was "his kingly neglect of trifles". He could ignore the little irritations that keep most people awake half the night. He could endure uncomfortable inns, the frustration of a lame horse, the cantankerousness of liverymen, with quiet poise. His major business was to preach the Gospel, and no mere details must be allowed to get in the way of his major business.

Most seriously of all, Martha's efficiency blocked her fellowship with Jesus. How singularly honoured was this woman that of all the homes in all the world and in all the centuries the earthly Jesus should have chosen her home in which to find rest and refreshment before setting out on the ordeal of his Passion and death! What a precious opportunity for personal communion with the living Christ of God, an opportunity envied and coveted by the saints and apostles of every age and generation! Yet Martha missed that opportunity. She was too busy in the kitchen, too encumbered with household duties, too enslaved to life's details.

So easily we allow the little things to come between us and God. "I could never go to church on Sunday mornings," says one housewife; "I have to stay home and cook dinner for the family." "Serve them a cold meal," we suggest, "or if you can afford it, invest in one of those automatic cookers with a time mechanism which does the work for you." "Heavens!" she exclaims, "I should just sit in church worrying if the gadget had really started, or if the joint might not be overdone." Thus do life's details blind us to what Jesus called the one thing that is needful, "that good part" which Mary chose when, realizing the uniqueness, the once-and-for-all ness of the occasion, she let the little things go by the board for one day and sat quietly at the feet of God's Christ.

In one of the most soul-searching Lent books ever written the Dean of Westminster* makes the all-important distinction between "perfection" and "perfectionism". "Perfectionism," he says, "can be a great scourge." It can result in "a deep anxiety about moral and other forms of attainment, overseverity to oneself, and censoriousness of others". It can lead not only to pride but often to various kinds of breakdown. That was Martha's soul-sickness which Jesus diagnosed with unerring accuracy. Christ comes as the Great Physician to heal not only the sick but the un-sick, those who, though sound of body and mind, suffer from moods which can do great harm to themselves and others. In this idiom, health denotes wholeness of personality, a blessed state which very

* Eric Abbott, *The Compassion of God and the Passion of Christ* (Geoffrey Bles, London, 1963), pp. 62–4.

few people enjoy. We know that all is not well so long as we harbour attitudes that make us miserable, stultify our relationships, distort our perspective and stand between us and God. In Martha, the petty perfectionist, some of us can see ourselves, knowing that what Jesus once said to her he says now to us, not as a sharp reprimand but as a healing word that speaks directly to the condition of our souls.

The story of Mary and Martha is one of the most exquisite in the Gospel. These two sisters do not contradict each other; they complement each other, as a friend of mine acknowledged when he christened his infant daughter "Marytha", a combination of the two names. To compare Mary and Martha would be no less impossible than comparing a rose with an orchid, or asking a child, "Whom do you love more, your father or your mother?" Each sister represents a very important and necessary outlook on life—Martha, the efficient one with her capacity for details; Mary, the contemplative one, sitting at the feet of Jesus. The full life, the healthy life combines both outlooks: on the one hand, a mind for little things; but on the other hand, a spiritual vision that redeems us from slavery to little things and enables us to live with the largest possible meaning and purpose.

One week-end I had the privilege of being a guest in the home of a woman whose Christian name is Mary but whose character combines that of both the Bethany sisters. Her husband is a man of distinction, so she has to do a great deal of official entertaining. Without full-time servants she manages a cavernously large home and does it with the utmost efficiency, never happier than when her thirteen grandchildren come to fill all the rooms. Never have I encountered a more gracious hostess, so solicitous for my comfort, not forgetting, as is so important in England, the hot-water bottle, the morning tea-tray, and even offering to polish my shoes. Yet by her conversation one soon realized that the details of housework do not enslave her mind which is as wide as the world. It did not astonish me to find on the crowded book-shelves some volumes which she has written on a subject about which she is an expert—voluntary social service. "How ever do you find time?" I asked her. "I make the time," she replied. "You see, I could easily become a slave to housework because I enjoy it so much, but one's life must be larger than the details of one's home and family."

What, then, is the cure for the spiritual dis-ease of pettiness? What shall we do when we find ourselves enslaved to details, tyrannized by trivialities and snowed under an avalanche of little things? We shall try to lead a more balanced life, stop being Marthas occasionally and sit with Mary at the feet of Jesus until his scale of values becomes ours and we begin to see life in its wholeness and, instead of striving to be perfectionists, become perfect in him. In practical terms this means periodic withdrawals from the busy world into the secret sanctuary of the soul, beginning each day or ending it, doing both perhaps, with a few moments of prayer and devotional reading; creating, as it were, a framework of eternity in which the picture of time shall be seen in its true perspective. To repeat some words of Jesus as we go about our daily work—"Is not life more than food, and the body more than clothing?"—can do much to banish troubling trifles and put them in their place. A simple prayer—"O Christ, give me your serenity"—will broaden our horizon. Least of all can we afford to refuse the weekly invitation to ascend the mountain of public worship where hymns, prayers, scripture, sermon and sacrament become a means of grace through which we approach Christ, see him in his transfigured glory and afterwards return to a life which has itself become transfigured.

CHAPTER IX

WITH A CROOKED CIVIL SERVANT

THE city of Jericho has to be seen to be believed. Set in the lush Jordan Valley and still called "The City of Palms", it resembles a huge green oasis in the midst of a brown, barren desert. When I visited Jericho I saw many relics of sacred history. I saw excavations of the walls which archaeologists tell us were destroyed by an earthquake about the year 1600 B.C., just the time when the children of Israel crossed the Jordan into the Promised Land. I saw Elisha's Fountain where by adding a few grains of salt the prophet turned bitter water into sweet. I saw the gaunt, craggy Mount of Temptation from which Jesus caught a view of the kingdoms that would be his if he transferred his allegiance from God to Satan. And in the very midst of the city at a junction of two streets I saw a sycamore tree, one of these typical eastern shade trees with a broad, short trunk and thick forked branches spreading out like a huge umbrella. As I stood there a moment and studied that tree, my imagination played a little drama based on an incident in the Gospels.

It was early morning many centuries ago, and the city still slept. Suddenly I noticed a man approaching the sycamore tree from the opposite direction, a man short in stature, carrying a bucket of water. He did not see me but with every appearance of knowing what he was doing he engaged in a most unorthodox procedure. First he put down the bucket. Then he began to gather and cast away the stones and branches and rubbish that lay around the foot of the tree. Having done this, he poured water on the roots and, gently caressing the trunk with his hands, stood silent as if in affectionate reminiscence and contemplation.

That was too much for my western curiosity. I came forward, coughed discreetly and opened my mouth as if to speak. Noticing me, the little man smiled, "I know what you're thinking," he said. "You are wondering if I have lost my head over a tree." He looked at the old sycamore. "Well, perhaps I do count this one rather worth preserving. It was here that I found Christ."

He picked up the empty bucket and walked over to me. "You are a stranger in Jericho," he said. "Welcome to our city. My name is Zacchaeus." I greeted him rather confusedly and muttered an apology for intruding on what had obviously been a ritual of remembrance and love. "Don't apologize," he replied, "I do this every morning. As I told you, it was here in this sycamore tree that I found Christ." My bewilderment increased. "You found him *up* in this tree?" Zacchaeus laughed, "I was up in the tree. *He* stood on the ground not far from where you are now standing at this moment. But, ridiculous as it sounds, I was up the tree. And," he added, "you can take that in a figurative as well as a literal sense."

The little man became serious. "This tree," he said, "changed my life. It redeemed my past, transformed the present and redirected the future. I climbed its branches one kind of a man and came down from its branches another kind of a man." He laid his hand on the trunk again. "I count this tree as sacred as the holy of holies in the Temple at Jerusalem." Then, observing my puzzled expression, he smiled again, a winsome, infectious smile. "Perhaps you would be interested in my story. But let us not linger here. The ground is damp and the air chill. Come home with me and share my morning meal."

We walked together through the city streets soon to be filled with the jostling crowds. But the hour was early, and as yet no sign of life disturbed the morning stillness. To me it felt like a holy stillness, a sacred spell, and I feared to break it with the grating sound of forced conversation. We didn't need to speak, this little Jew and I. Somehow we both sensed a community of understanding, a language of minds that made the spoken word unnecessary.

Zacchaeus seemed grateful that I chose to walk beside him in silence. He did notice that I looked rather closely at a pretentious house set back from the road, obviously the home of wealthy people. "That was mine once," he remarked a bit curtly but he said nothing more until we had passed through the city's business district, beyond all the large buildings, and had made our way along several side-streets to a house so small and modest that I gasped at its contrast with the one we had passed a few minutes earlier.

We shared a simple meal on that morning so vivid in my imagination. The fresh and dried fruits we followed with cold, sparkling water which Zacchaeus had drawn as we came by the town well. My hunger abated, I could contain myself no longer. "Zacchaeus," I said, "your hospitality has been most gracious, and I thank you for it; but I have a thousand questions to ask you, questions about the sycamore tree, the big house and now this modest home. I know you have guessed already that I am a Christian, just as you are. I too, have found Christ, accepted him as my Lord and Saviour. There was nothing dramatic about my Christian experience, perhaps because I grew into it naturally, or because I haven't yet paid a high enough price. But I can see that with you the whole thing has been real and vital. Something tremendous has happened to you, and I want to hear about it." "You shall hear about it," he replied. "You are quite right. My experience of Christ was tremendous. You see," he said quite matter-of-factly, "I was a publican, a chief publican."

My mouth dropped open in astonishment. Zacchaeus a publican? This charming, courteous, apparently guileless little man—Chief of the Jericho Publicans? It didn't seem

possible. Publicans were the most unprincipled, most schem-
ing, most ruthless members of Jewish society, far more dis-
honest and cruel than the thieves and brigands who infested
the Jericho Road. A publican was a man who had bartered
his soul.

The Roman government required a certain *per capita* tax
from all its subjects, even the impoverished Jews. It farmed
out the business of collecting these hated taxes to chief publicans, usually "quisling" Jews who in turn farmed it out to
other publicans, also "quisling" Jews. The chief publican had
to pay the Roman government the required tax but he was
permitted as substantial a rake-off for himself and for his
underlings as he could, by the force of Roman arms, squeeze
out of his defenceless fellow-citizens. No decent person would
associate with a publican; society rated him lower than cut-
throats and robbers and adulterers and brothel-keepers. A
man had to be the lowest kind of character to engage in this
despicable business of extorting taxes for the Romans.

Do you wonder then that I stared in astonishment at
Zacchaeus? If this man had once been a publican then he had
indeed been born again. Nothing else could describe it. "Yes,
I know it must seem fantastic to you," he said, "but it's true.
I was not only a tax-collector; I was the most unscrupulous
kind of tax-collector, as many of my fellow-citizens still re-
mind me every day with their sneers and their snobbery. But
God knows I deserve that."

"What changed you, Zacchaeus?" I asked him. "Jesus
Christ changed me," he replied simply. "Yes," I said, "but
even Christ cannot redeem a man unless he wants to be redeemed. What kindled within your heart a willingness to be
changed? What prompted you to put yourself in the way of
Christ? Had the pressure of social ostracism worn you down?
Were you conscience-stricken about being a tax-collector?"
"No," replied Zacchaeus, "I had long since stifled my sense
of shame. It bothered me at first to take food out of hungry
children's mouths, but any evil can be rationalized if you

keep at it long enough. All you have to do is to take a good look at the people around you, especially the religious ones whose piety covers a multitude of respectable sins far more odious than mine. I reminded myself again and again that someone had to collect taxes, that every man has to look out for himself and that certainly no-one would support me if I suddenly became virtuous and gave up the business. No, it wasn't a sense of shame that put me in the way of Christ."

"What was it then?" I asked him. Zacchaeus remained silent a moment. Then he said, "Loneliness, I suppose, emptiness, boredom, futility. I possessed everything that most men want—properties, money, servants, securities, but I paid too high a price for them. The Master explained it to me when he said that I had gained the whole world and lost my own soul. Certainly I had lost the things I most wanted—peace, dignity, self-respect. I felt alienated from my inheritance as a Jew, alienated from God, alienated from my fellow-men, alienated from myself. What should have been a paradise for me had become a living hell." For a long time neither of us spoke. Zacchaeus went over to the door, opened it and let the morning sunshine flood the room with its radiance. "But it's all changed now," he said with a smile, returning to his chair, "all changed because of a sycamore tree."

"Tell me about the sycamore tree," I asked him, "I have been waiting to hear about it for the last two hours." Zacchaeus replied, "You remember the large house we passed this morning, the one with the porch surrounded by great pillars? That house belonged to me. I built it with my extorted wealth. One morning, as I was sitting in the porch computing taxes, I heard a commotion out on the street. I looked and saw a great crowd of people running and talking excitedly. I called a servant and asked, 'What's all the noise about?' 'Don't you know?' he replied. 'Jesus of Nazareth is passing through Jericho on his way to Jerusalem.' Jesus of Nazareth! I had heard that name before. Who hadn't? I had heard how he went up and down the country telling people about God and goodness, how he healed the sick, how he forgave sins, how he got into trouble with the authorities so that they were planning to arrest him and how he had attracted a company of disciples, one of them a publican like myself. That very morning he had opened the eyes of a blind beggar in our own city. Everyone was talking about it. Jesus of Nazareth! Suddenly I flung down my financial tablet, threw a cloak over my shoulders and rushed out into the street and followed the crowd. What possessed me I don't know; I only know that I had a consuming desire at that moment to see this Jesus of Nazareth."

"Is that where the sycamore tree came in?" I asked him. "Yes," replied Zacchaeus, "that's where the sycamore tree came in. When I reached the place where Jesus was expected to pass I found the road lined with a crowd of people ten deep. Even had I been a tall man I could never have hoped to see over them, and you may be sure that when some of them recognized me they formed a solid phalanx, deliberately holding me back and blocking my view. Well, that made me all the more determined, and suddenly I noticed the tree with its broad, comfortable perch fairly inviting an occupant. What could be more perfect? I acted quickly and, grasping one of the low, overhanging limbs, I pulled myself up to a place where I had a good view of the road. Needless to say, my undignified behaviour attracted ridicule and abuse. I could hear the cries of derision. 'Look at that old publican and extortioner! Robber of widows and orphans! May he burn in Gehenna for ever!' Some of the street urchins began flinging rocks, and they might have hit me except that a shrill shout suddenly arrested the crowd's attention as a little procession came into view.

"I mean a little procession. It amounted to nothing, and I couldn't help wondering what all the fuss was about and why this Jesus of Nazareth had caused such a stir throughout Galilee and Judea. Surely all the reports about him had been exaggerated. He seemed like an ordinary-looking man. There were no banners, no trumpets, no insignia of rank; and after him came an entourage of twelve equally ordinary-looking men, most of them peasants and fishermen. I began to feel like a fool for allowing myself to become the victim of mob hysteria. I started searching for ways of getting down out of this tree—unnoticed.

"Then, all of a sudden, Jesus turned his head. Up to that point he had scarcely noticed the crowd, just moved forward with his eyes focused straight in front of him as if he were going somewhere, as if an appointment awaited him in Jerusalem, an appointment for which he must not be late. But he turned his head. For the first time I could see his face and in that moment I knew the secret of his magnetism. His eyes held me like a vice. Everything else—the crowd, the sky, the buildings, the tree, the procession, faded from view. I saw nothing but the face of that man. I had never seen such a face—so strong yet so gentle, so sad yet so joyous, so troubled yet so serene, so stern yet so kind. How can I describe it save to say that it was the cleanest, purest, noblest, finest face I had ever seen?

"Suddenly I knew that it was more than the face of a man. It was the face of Man as God created him and before sin disfigured him. And that face judged me. In that moment I really saw for the first time the loathsomeness and despicableness of my life of greed and extortion. I had hardened myself to society's censure, but this man judged me without saying a word. He simply reflected my face as God first created it, my face as I secretly longed to behold it every morning in a mirror. Something within me went out to meet this man. At once I knew that more than anything in the world I wanted to talk with Jesus, spend time in his presence and draw from him the courage to do what I must do if life could ever again become tolerable and meaningful. Talk with him? Spend time with him? What was I dreaming about? Can the Devil spend time with God? No, there was no hope for me.

I had reached the point of no return. I just couldn't look at that face any longer.

"Then he looked up at me. He stopped the little procession, ignored the crowds and looked at the sycamore tree where I sat ridiculously perched among the branches. 'Zacchaeus,' he called.. (I couldn't have been more surprised if the tree itself had spoken.) 'Zacchaeus!' (How did he know my name? He had never seen me before, yet he spoke as if he had always known me, as if he had walked down the street for the express purpose of meeting me at this tree.) 'Zacchaeus, make haste and come down, for I must stay at your house today.'

"A gasp of horror went up from the crowd. Did he know what he was saying? Nothing could have done more to discredit Jesus in Jericho than his willingness to break bread in the house of a chief publican. And that he himself should have proposed it! I wonder that the people of our city didn't crucify him there and then. Yet there could be no mistaking what he had said—'Zacchaeus, make haste and come down, for I must stay at your house today.' I could hardly believe my ears! Never in all the world would I have summoned up enough courage to extend such an invitation. I had been praying to a forgotten God for the opportunity of a few moments' conversation with Jesus, and here he was offering to be a guest in my home.

"What I didn't know was that God had sent Jesus to single out people like me. You call me Zacchaeus, but I am really every man who has ever been up the tree of his own moral failure, hating himself for it, longing to be different but lacking the will and the courage to come down. God sent Jesus, and Jesus always takes the initiative. He doesn't care what we have been or what we are. He sees us for what God intended us to become and, if we make the slightest effort to put ourselves in the way of him, he takes the initiative and graciously reaches out to help us."

At that point Zacchaeus stopped. "Forgive me," he said, "I have been talking for a long time, boring you, perhaps, or keeping you from some appointment. But at least you know now why that old sycamore is so sacred to me, why I count it so worth preserving. It was there that I found Jesus Christ." "But you mustn't stop," I said. "Please go on. What happened after Jesus called you down from the tree? Did he go home with you? What did you and he talk about?"

"Well, that's the odd thing," replied Zacchaeus. "The conversation didn't go the way I had expected it to go at all. I rather thought that after we had finished our dinner Jesus would examine my soul in the way that a physician examines a patient's body. I thought he would be very stern and say, 'Now see here, Zacchaeus, this life of thievery hasn't been good enough. It's wrong morally. What are you going to do about it?' But he didn't talk that way at all. He asked me to tell him about my early years, my parents, my boyhood, the dreams I cherished before getting involved in extortion and crime. He talked about God as naturally as man talks about his father, of how God is like a Father, slow to anger, of great kindness and always ready to forgive. He talked about the history of our people and of how the hopes of the prophets and psalmists, the hopes of God's Kingdom will one day be fulfilled. He talked about what he called 'eternal life', a way of living so rich and full and abundant that it survives even the grave. But most of all he treated me like a human being. He was neither impressed by my wealth nor shocked by the way I had acquired it. He just gave me his friendship, and I knew that more than anything else in the world I wanted to keep that friendship.

"But I knew something more. I knew that to keep his friendship I must pay a price. Graciously he had said, 'Zacchaeus, make haste and come down, for I must stay at your house today'; but it has to be a certain kind of house that can receive Jesus as a guest. Some things will not live in his presence, and one has to choose between him and them.

There and then I made my choice. Suddenly, like the bursting of a dam, I cried out 'Behold, Lord, the half of my goods I give to the poor, and if I have defrauded anyone of anything, I restore it fourfold.' And Jesus just smiled and said, 'Today is salvation come to this house.' "

It was getting late now and time I took my leave of Zacchaeus. As I rose to go, he said, "Does that answer your question about my move from the big house to this modest house? I became a comparatively poor man after I accepted Christ. It took nearly everything I owned to make good that large promise; and don't forget I no longer have a profession. You see," he said slowly, "in loyalty to Christ you may have to change not only your house but also your way of making a living. In fact, you may have to change nearly everything in your life of any real importance."

"I know that," I replied, "and that is why I want to ask you this one last question. Do you ever regret your decision?" "Occasionally," Zacchaeus answered with candour. "It isn't easy to eat porridge after you have been used to the choicest of meats. Also I become discouraged when people persistently refuse to believe in my conversion and judge me by what I was rather than by what I am now. Then, too," he went on, "you may have heard that the Romans crucified our Christ and that they persecute us for following him. But the tree gives me courage." "The tree?" I asked. "Yes," he replied, "the tree. I often think of it, gaunt and naked in winter, and of how it seems miraculously to come alive under the warm spring skies. It is a symbol of *his* resurrection from the dead, and of mine too. Call it fulfilment, if you like, the bringing out of all in it that is worth fulfilling. Christ does that for us. He makes us into something we can never be without him, and what he does for us is worth more than any price we can possibly pay."

CHAPTER X

WITH A PILLAR OF THE ESTABLISHMENT

It must have been pleasant for Jesus relaxing on a Jerusalem roof-top under the Judean night sky. All day long he and the disciples had tramped the dusty roads under the scorching heat of a pitiless sun. Engulfed by an ocean of suffering humanity, not once had he paused in his compassionate work of teaching and healing to seek shade or refreshment for himself. But now blessed night had fallen, and while the city slept, and while his disciples took their rest in the room below, Jesus retreated to the roof-top to renew his strength. It would be very peaceful. A cool, refreshing breeze caressed his cheek. In the distance he saw the Mount of Olives floodlighted by a silvery moon; above him the myriads of stars glittered like diamonds in the sky. The Master cherished these moments of solitude, these brief withdrawals from the busy world when his soul sought sustenance in quiet communion with God.

Suddenly a sound breaks the stillness—a rustling of garments, footsteps on the stairs that lead up from the street. Who can it be at this midnight hour? Some broken wretch, perhaps, denied sleep by a nagging pain of body or soul? Jesus stares in astonishment at the figure that emerges from the shadows. We share his astonishment, because this is no unfamiliar figure. Clothed in the garments of first-century Palestine, yet he bears a curious resemblance to someone we meet every day. In fact, as he approaches more closely, so that we can see his face in the full light of the moon, we have the uncanny feeling that we are looking into a mirror. We see ourselves in the nocturnal visitor, we hear our own voice speaking from his lips; and, as we listen to the dialogue that follows, we begin to understand that here is a crucial encounter in which we are not spectators but participants. Jesus Christ is the same yesterday, today and for ever; and this man who came to him by night represents us.

He represents us in the type of person that he was. The New Testament calls him Nicodemus. From the account of this interview and from his further appearances in the Gospel drama we know something about him. We can judge from the evidence that he was comparatively wealthy, an aristocrat who belonged to one of the distinguished Jerusalem families. He was a Pharisee, belonging to that most exclusive religious sect whose members pledged themselves to spend all their lives observing every detail of the sacred law. We must not allow their hostility towards Jesus to obscure the fact that in many ways the Pharisees were the finest people, the most morally upright in the whole country. The name "Pharisee" means "The Separated One"; and that describes him exactly—a man who separated himself from the world's pleasures in order to lead a life of exemplary devotion and goodness. Of Nicodemus we know also that he was a ruler of the Jews, which meant that he held a seat in the Sanhedrin, the supreme court of seventy members responsible for safeguarding religious ortho-doxy and exercising religious jurisdiction over every Jew in the world.

Do you wonder, then, that Jesus greeted him with astonish-ment? He should, of course, have felt highly flattered. Up to this point his influence had been more or less restricted to common folk—peasants, farmers, fishermen, small merchants —those with no social or economic standing in the community. Nicodemus represented his first point of contact with society's upper crust; and what made it all the more remarkable was the fact that this pillar of the Jewish Establishment had taken the initiative and come to see him.

We might grasp the drama of the situation by imagining

some young nonconformist lay preacher from the provinces coming to London's East End and drawing huge crowds to hear him in the pubs and on the street corners. Under the impact of his magnetic ministry hardened criminals are converted to goodness, fallen women lifted to purity, and incurably sick people healed. To multitudes, who would never step inside a church, this freelance evangelist mediates the forgiveness and saving love of God. Of course, he never reaches beyond the circle of working people. Class barriers exclude him from the circle of the social, the cultural and the ecclesiastical élite. Late one night, however, a limousine draws up outside the house in Whitechapel where he is staying. Out of it steps a pillar of the Establishment, resplendent in clerical collar and gaiters. One of the country's leading bishops, a member of the House of Lords, has taken the initiative and come to seek an interview with him.

But why exaggerate? Nicodemus is a more familiar figure than that. In secular society he represents the solid citizens, the eminently respectable, who normally believe that they have a built-in strength of character to which Christ can add nothing. There are many intelligent, charming, decent people who are not religious because they honestly feel no need of religion. They look upon the practice of piety as a substitute for worldly success, the refuge of the poor, the weak, the morally degraded. They regard religion as a kind of ambulance, the Church as a hospital and Christ as a Physician to whom we turn as a last resort in crisis or old age. These people are not anti-religious. They think the ambulance service is a good thing. They may even contribute to the upkeep of the hospital and honour it with their presence on stated occasions; but preach Christ to them, and they will reply patiently in Christ's own words, "Those who are well have no need of a physician, but those who are sick."

Even within the Church we can find a counterpart of Nicodemus. Here he represents what has come to be known as the "in-group"; it includes those who have inherited the

Christian Faith and have never had reason to doubt it. These modern pillars of orthodoxy, who pay pew rents and worship regularly and keep the wheels of ecclesiastical machinery in motion, almost take it as an insult when you ask them if they have really experienced a first-hand encounter with the radical Christ of God. "We have been Christians all our lives!" they exclaim. On one occasion, when I preached about the Nicodemus incident to a prosperous congregation, taking as my text the key verse, "Except a man be born again, he cannot see the Kingdom of God," those well dressed people stared at me in frank amazement. "This has nothing to do with us," they seemed silently to be saying. "Preach your old-fashioned Gospel outside to the derelicts and the unbelievers. We are the converted!"

From every point of view it does seem surprising that Nicodemus should have sought a personal audience with Jesus. In a word, he represents the people who equate religion with respectability and he represents those who equate vital Christian experience with membership in the Church. For that reason we can the more easily identify ourselves with him and for that reason we ought to look closely at this crucial encounter, knowing it to be *our* encounter with the living Christ. In the type of person that he was Nicodemus represents us.

He represents us also in the manner of his approach to Jesus. The Master himself was no doubt prepared for it, but we cannot help contrasting Nicodemus with countless others who approached Jesus in the attitude of supplication. Sick people clutched his garments, threw themselves on his mercy and implored him to show compassion and restore them to health. Zacchaeus, the wealthy tax-collector, made himself a laughing-stock by climbing a sycamore tree just to catch a glimpse of the Saviour of his soul. Even the Rich Young Ruler ran breathlessly up to him, flung himself at his feet and cried out, "Good Master, what must I do to inherit eternal life?" All of these came humbly to Jesus. They saw in him something that they desperately needed. They recognized that he could do for them what they could not do for themselves and without pride they pleaded with him to help them.

Not so Nicodemus. He did not show himself a supplicant. He came to discuss religion with the young Physician, not to take his medicine. Though displaying a certain deference, yet by his opening words he made it clear that he placed himself on an equal footing with Jesus: "Rabbi, we know that you are a teacher come from God; for no-one can do these signs that you do, unless God is with him." It gives substance to the theory that Nicodemus may, in fact, have come officially on behalf of the religious authorities. Though appearing to ignore Jesus, the Pharisees would certainly be aware of his phenomenal impact on the popular mind. Already the people were beginning to acclaim him as the long-awaited Messiah. It could not be true, of course, but there was only one way to find out. We can imagine the Pharisees, after much debate, delegating one of their number, a man of judicial temper and kindly disposition, to visit Jesus secretly and bring back a report on the basis of which they would either support him or take steps to get rid of him. This could explain why Nicodemus introduced himself by saying not, "*I* know," but "*We* know that you are a teacher come from God."

It has been said of the Pharisees that, when they prayed, they approached God as a shareholder approaches a corporation in which he holds a considerable block of stock. Does that not describe the approach of some church members? Every pastor observes with sadness that the people whom he seems least able to help are the very people who play the most active part in the life of his church. They become partners with him in a religious enterprise; they tend to view him as a hired business manager who either supports or opposes their ideas and schemes. They meet him as a spiritual equal—which may indeed be justified—but it does block his spiritual influence when he tries to exercise his priestly office toward them. Unconsciously, perhaps, they may even take the same attitude towards Christ and think, not in terms of what he can do for them but rather in terms of what they can do for his Church.

The Bishop of Woolwich is not the first modern theologian to propose that man "come of age" needs a radically revised image of God. In the 1940's an American Jewish rabbi, Joshua Loth Liebman, wrote a book entitled *Peace of Mind*.* Though it accounted for many sales, the title is misleading, because the author actually introduces what he calls "A New God Idea for America". He insists that the traditional concept of God is out of date and that Americans must construct a new image that will fit their contemporary situation. He says that the old picture of our relationship with God in terms of the powerless, poverty-stricken motifs in European culture simply will not satisfy the growing, self-confident character of America. Writes Rabbi Liebman:

> "We must be brave enough to declare that every culture must create its own God idea rather than rely upon outworn tradition . . . America should come to its God idea not through a feeling of helplessness, but through a feeling of confidence. The religion of the future, for the first time, may become a partnership religion in which men will not only *say*, but will *feel* that they are indispensable to God."

That was how Nicodemus approached Jesus, and there are two things to be said about it. On the one hand it shows a certain nobility; on the other hand it shows a pride that almost borders on idolatry. To conceive of God as a kindly, co-operative senior-partner is simply to revise him in our own image and to ignore the fact that he is *God* who sits, as the prophet wrote, "above the circle of the earth; and its inhabitants are like grasshoppers". To approach Christ as a spiritual equal and to regard him as the mere Founder of a

* Simon and Schuster, Inc., New York, 1946.

religious enterprise were to ignore the fact that he is the *Christ*, the Son of God, the Saviour in whom, if we believe, we shall not perish but have eternal life.

Nicodemus represents us in his ignorance of his own real problem. We wonder why this solid citizen did not approach Jesus during the day but came to him furtively under the shadow of night. Commentators have offered their theories; but we cannot escape the conclusion that for obvious reasons Nicodemus did not want to be seen either by the common people or by his colleagues in the Sanhedrin. Subsequent events seem to indicate that he came not officially but on his own. Perhaps he had heard Jesus preach and seen him perform miracles and each time had come away persuaded that, whoever or whatever else he might be, this young ex-carpenter from Nazareth stood in a unique relationship with God. There was no question that Jesus possessed something, a quality of life for which he, Nicodemus, despite all his wealth and social prominence, had passionately longed but which he had never been able to find. An irresistible urge drove him to seek Jesus out and talk with him privately. Behind all his veneer of piety and respectability was an aching void that Christ alone could fill.

Jesus saw that immediately and came directly to the point. To the rather pompous introduction, "Rabbi, we know that you are a teacher come from God," Jesus answered incisively, "Truly, truly, I say to you, unless one is born anew he cannot see the Kingdom of God." He was saying in effect, "Look Nicodemus, I know why you have come, so let us not waste time on generalities. Let us be personal rather than philosophical. Let us settle your problems before trying to settle the problems of theology. You want to talk about my relationship with God. Well, the truth is that we shall both be talking different languages until you stand in that same relationship, the relationship of obedience which acknowledges God as King and yourself as subject. To do that you have to

E

change not your ideas but your life. You have to be born again."

Then follows a fascinating dialogue which you can read for yourself in the third chapter of John's Gospel, a dialogue that becomes almost amusing in its interplay of moods. As a devout Jew, Nicodemus understood clearly enough the whole idea of re-birth. The rabbis described a Gentile converted to Judaism as "a child newly born". Indeed, this re-birth into the religious community of Israel became the proselyte's only valid passport into the Kingdom of God. It would shock Nicodemus to hear from Jesus that a son of Abraham must enter the Kingdom on the same terms as the despised heathen. Moreover, the idea would offend him personally. To be sure, publicans and prostitutes needed to make a radical new beginning in life, but what business had Jesus putting him in a class with society's offscourings? Yet, despite his alternating sincerity and bluff, Nicodemus must have sensed that Jesus had exposed his real problem. Jew or no Jew, religious or not religious, he did, in fact, need to be re-born spiritually but he refused to face up to it, and in his refusal he represents us.

Every spiritual counsellor has tried to help some Nicodemus who professed to be puzzled or perturbed about religion but would not recognize himself as his real problem. A woman came to see me because she was dreadfully worried about her husband. "He seems to have lost his faith," she burst out. "He won't go to church any more and he ridicules me and the children when we go. He has become so unpleasant around the house that I fear for the future of our marriage." "Why not tell your own minister?" I suggested. "I can't," she replied, "because he is largely to blame for the trouble. For a long time our pulpit was vacant, so my husband, as senior layman, pretty well ran things around the church. We called a minister recently, and now *he* wants to be in charge of the church." "Is that so unusual?" I murmured. She looked surprised and continued, "It hurts my husband, because . . . well . . . he's never been very successful, and his authority

at the church made him feel important. He has become so
bitter that he says that he won't go back to the church and
that he doesn't even believe in God." "You have cause to be
worried," I told her. "This is indeed a serious situation,
especially as far as your family life is concerned. You say that
your husband no longer believes in God. Is that the fault of
the minister and the church?" "My husband says so," she
replied honestly, "but I know that he has only himself to
blame."

The trouble with the people whom Nicodemus represents
is that the very qualities and relationships which should lead
them to Christ become an obstacle in the way of vital Christian experience. When Nicodemus professed puzzlement about
the renewing power of the Holy Spirit, Jesus asked, perhaps
with a smile, "Are you a teacher of Israel, and yet you do not
understand this?" Jesus knew that *because* he was a teacher
of Israel, a solid citizen, a leader in the Church, Nicodemus
did not understand. If he had been a sinner, a tax-collector,
a social outcast, he would have known that he did, in fact,
need to be born again, but piety and respectability not only
blinded him to his real problem; in his case, as in our case,
perhaps, they became his real problem.

Nicodemus represents us in what he missed. We see in him
the type of man who can achieve honour in church and community and still miss the greatest thing in life. Not that he
came away unaffected by his crucial encounter with Christ.
Months later, when the Sanhedrin decided to do away with
Jesus, Nicodemus sprang weakly to his defence, "Does our
Law judge a man without first giving him a hearing and without learning what he does?" The protest went unheeded, and
the murderous plot reached its climax on Calvary. In the end
the best that Nicodemus could do for Jesus was to help take
his mangled corpse down from the Cross and provide the
materials for an expensive burial.

It might have turned out so differently. Given the chance

to re-write the story, we should tell of a soul-shaking conversion on that Jerusalem roof-top. We should picture Nicodemus coming away from his crucial encounter with Jesus a changed man, ready to use all his influence and to sacrifice all his wealth and prestige for the sake of his new Master. His name would figure prominently in the *Acts of the Apostles* as one who proclaimed fearlessly the good news of the risen Christ. Yet in all probability he never knew that God raised Jesus from the dead. After the burial in Joseph's garden we never hear the name of Nicodemus again. We know that he admired Jesus but we also know that he did not become a Christian.

So it happens to many respectable people. They admire Jesus, they go to his church, they do what they can for him, they encounter Christ in worship and sacrament, but with no real change in their lives, no radical experience that empowers and transforms them and lifts them above the best pagans. They miss the greatest gift that Christ can offer them; and just how great it is came home to me in a letter which I received recently from a fine, attractive girl whom many years ago I prepared for church membership. Writing to tell me that she has just offered herself as a missionary, she says:

"Last Spring I received the Baptism of the Holy Spirit. It has been the most important occurrence in my life. Nothing has changed me so radically. I have always been a person of many and varied moods . . . ecstatic one day, and horribly depressed the next. I have 'levelled off', as it were; and although my frame of mind is not always on an even keel, I no longer get upset or worried. I am no longer frustrated or depressed. I can't really tell you how this has changed me. Hardly a day goes by without someone expressing how much at peace I look, act and speak. I thank God that he never intended the Christian life to be one of continual trying and striving. It is abundant living by trusting in his Son and by being obedient."

Inevitably we contrast the man who came to Jesus at midnight with the man whom Christ met at midday. Saul of Tarsus was a Pharisee, morally upright, eminently respectable, fanatically religious. He never knew Jesus in the flesh, but when the living Christ encountered him on the road to Damascus there was no discussion of religion, no parrying of words, only an act of total and absolute surrender—"Lord, what wilt thou have me to do?" A new birth took place in *that* crucial encounter. There the old life ended, and there the new life began. Saul the Pharisee became Paul the Apostle. That is why Paul in his letters dwells unremittingly on the need of this miracle of death and resurrection which Christ effects in the life of every man who surrenders to him in faith and obedience. "If any man be in Christ, he is a new creature; old things are passed away, behold, all things are become new." It happened to Paul himself. It happened to the girl who wrote that letter. It could have happened to Nicodemus. It can happen to you.

CHAPTER XI

WITH A MAN OF MEANS

THE age of disillusionment is always characterized by a general feeling of restlessness. We seem to be living in such an age today. Never has western society had it so good. Never have we been richer in material possessions, more affluent in the means of physical comfort or more privileged in the opportunities for education and pleasure. We ought to be the most contented, most relaxed, most well-adjusted generation in history; but we are not. Although they have everything that should make them happy, a great many people feel empty, restless, dissatisfied and bored. They know that something is lacking, something they cannot rationally define; and that is the reason, perhaps, why they search for it in irrational ways. A recent survey of the gambling craze in Britain concludes that most people who frequent bingos and betting shops do so not because they need money but because they need excitement. They know, however dimly, that eating, sleeping, working, procreating and dying do not add up to life; and that is what they are looking for—*life*.

Let us see ourselves, then, in a man whom we have come to know as "The Rich Young Ruler". Whether that description fits him accurately we cannot be sure because it represents a composite picture drawn from his appearance in three of the Gospels. On one feature only the Gospel writers agree—he was rich. The artist, George Frederick Watts, portrays this in a famous painting which hangs in the Tate Gallery. The man's clothing, his silk sleeves and turban, the velvet and fur of his mantle, the rings on his fingers and the elaborate chain about his shoulders—all indicate the possession of wealth. Not only was he rich, but if we add the other features in the Gospel story, we can assume that, like Nicodemus, he was both morally upright and a pillar of the religious Establishment. He had everything that a man wanted in those days, everything, it would seem, except life. The pallid pleasures and short satisfactions purchasable by his perishable riches did not satisfy him. He wanted something more, a quality of life so full, so vibrant and so replete with meaning that nothing, not even the grave, could diminish its power.

One day he saw it, this very life for which he had thirsted as an animal thirsts for water in the dry season. He, the rich aristocrat, recognized in a penniless prophet from Nazareth the goal of all his searching. That was always the secret of the Master's magnetism. He did not preach people into the Kingdom of God, nor did he bulldoze them with miracles. His personal character spoke louder than his words and works. It was a character on fire with life and it drew men as only a fire does draw them, men of unclouded vision who saw in Jesus the perfect revelation of that eternal life for which they believed that God had created them. Like many another, the Rich Young Ruler pleaded with Jesus to share the secret, "Good Teacher, what must I do to inherit eternal life?"

It was one of the most important incidents in the personal ministry of Jesus, so vividly memorable to the disciples and so timeless in its teaching value that three of the Gospel writers record it with only the most minor variations. The story ends on a tragic note, but that is the very feature which brings it close to real life and compels us to examine it, not only as an historical incident but as a pattern of every man's encounter, perhaps our own crucial encounter with the living Christ of God.

Look briefly at the manner of this man's approach to Jesus. He came running—which was not a very dignified thing for someone in his position to do, but it bespoke a sense of eagerness and urgency. Kneeling at the feet of Jesus, he panted,

"Good Teacher . . . ," but almost before he could get his question out, Jesus threw cold water over his enthusiasm and froze him in his tracks, "Why do you call me good? No-one is good but God alone." There was reason for this sharp reprimand. No Jew addressed a rabbi as "Good Teacher" except in flattery, and Jesus was having none of that. He had come to mediate God, not to usurp God's glory; and it is a pity that the Church and especially the Church's leaders have not always been prepared to learn from him. Too often we confuse real religion with emotional attachment to some person, perhaps a gifted preacher or a devoted pastor. In fact, it is a form of idolatry which quickly crumbles when our idol passes from the scene. The true servant of God never covets human loyalty and adoration. His supreme ambition is to efface himself and bind men to God. Our Lord was doing that when he said, in effect, to the Rich Young Ruler, "No flattery! Don't call me good. Keep that word for God." Having settled that point, he probably added, "Now repeat your question."

The ruler repeated his question, "What must I do to inherit eternal life?" — an inquiry typical of the legalistic mind which assumes that eternal life, the life which God alone gives, can be earned by something that we "do", some act or series of acts that we perform. Years ago a Jewish gentleman came to my vestry. He had attended a funeral which I conducted and had been impressed with the certainty of our Christian hope of life everlasting. "I should like to have this certainty," he said. "I own a thriving business. I have been good to my family. I am an honest man, and religious. People call me philanthropic. But I haven't many more years to live. What must I do to possess your assurance that life does not end with the grave?" Jesus would have told him, as he told the Rich Young Ruler, that he was on the wrong road. Eternal life does not come as the reward of meritorious deeds but rather as a gift of Divine grace that grows out of our total relationship with God.

It is significant, however, that first of all, Jesus answered the ruler on his own terms. To the question, "What must I do . . .?", Jesus replied, "You know the commandments"; then he catalogued some of the God-given laws that govern man's duty to his fellow-man. Here again it is a pity that the Church has not always allowed itself to be instructed by Jesus. Recently our thinking has been confused by the writings of some avant-garde theologians who tell us that the Christian ethic contains no commandments; it goes beyond morality and requires only that we love our neighbours. These writers do not understand Jesus correctly, else they would remember that Jesus pointed to love as the fulfilment of the law, not as the substitute for it. He told men to love, but first he told them to obey the age-old commandments of God—"Thou shalt not kill, thou shalt not steal, thou shalt not commit adultery." In the teaching of Jesus love gives morality a new inwardness, a new motivation; it does not abrogate morality. Indeed much of the confusion and restlessness of our age may stem from a bad conscience; it may be due to the fact that people like to regard themselves as having graduated from morality when in fact they have hardly reached the primary stages.

The Rich Young Ruler *had* reached the primary stages. He passed the test with flying colours. To every question on the moral examination paper he replied confidently, "Teacher, all these things I have observed from my youth." He had kept every rule—do this, abstain from that, perform the other thing, pull the lever and "I score!" But he hadn't scored. He had run the whole gamut of self-salvation and drawn a blank, a dull, dismal, discouraging blank. In spite of his moral perfectionism, the life that he so eagerly sought, the timeless, transcendent life visible in Jesus, had eluded him. Though his earthly cup overflowed, he still said to himself, "This isn't enough." So what had he forgotten? What had he left out? What more could he do?

Abraham Lincoln once said that too many people consider themselves Christians simply because they behave decently enough to stay out of prison. The observance of negative morality does keep us out of prison but it does not admit us into the Kingdom of God. Jesus told that to the Rich Young Ruler. He said, in effect, "Observing the law will make you an upright, decent citizen of Israel; but it will not qualify you for eternal life." William Barclay* helps us to understand this answer when he defines eternal life as the life such as God himself lives, the life that is characteristic of God. The great characteristic of God is that he loves and gives. Therefore, the life that we so restlessly seek, the life of happiness, joy, satisfaction, peace of mind and serenity of heart, will be found not by manicuring our morals but by reproducing God's own attitude of sacrificial generosity to our fellow-men. That was the Rich Young Ruler's deficiency. He had obeyed God only in a negative sense. He had kept the Commandments. He had not murdered or stolen or committed adultery. He had never harmed anybody but neither, apparently, had he ever helped anybody. He lacked one thing in order to capture the life of God made visible in Jesus, one surpassing quality—the quality of self-negating love.

Dostoievski wrote a classic story about a woman who died and was told that she would be taken to heaven if she could remember one unselfish act that she had performed while on earth. She could remember only one—a withered carrot that she had given to a beggar. So down the limitless space that separates heaven from hell the carrot was lowered on a slender string. Desperately she grasped it and slowly began to rise. Suddenly she felt a weight holding her back and, looking down, she saw other tormented souls clinging to her and hoping to rise with her. "Let go!" she cried. "This is *my* carrot." At that point the string broke, and still clutching her precious carrot, the woman fell down into the pains of hell.

That story speaks to the condition of many people who complain of being empty, restless, dissatisfied and bored.

* The Daily Study Bible, *Gospel of Matthew*, Vol. 2 (The St. Andrew Press, Edinburgh, 1957), pp. 235–8.

Eternal life eludes them, because never once have they performed a genuinely sacrificial act, a deed of kindness that was
not prompted by some hidden motive of self-interest. They
have lived only for themselves. Like the Rich Young Ruler
they take too much for granted when they boast, "All these
things I have observed from my youth", as though to say
off-handedly, "I have brushed my teeth every day since I was
a boy." To be sure, they have observed the rules of morality
but only in a negative and legalistic sense. Had they observed these rules in the positive and wider sense that Jesus
interpreted them—never lusting after a woman's body, never
harbouring murderous thoughts, never spreading their own
tables while poor men starve, never conniving at false gossip,
never bringing heartache to their parents—then it would indeed require only one crowning gesture of generosity to make
their lives perfect. No longer would they search restlessly for
the life of God because in large measure they would already
possess that unselfish, outgoing life. They would not need to
ask the Rich Young Ruler's timeless question, "What do I
still lack?"

They ask it nevertheless, and Jesus answers them as he
answered the Rich Young Ruler, "You lack one thing; go,
sell what you have, and give to the poor, and you will have
treasure in heaven; and come, follow me." We are struck at
once by what seems like the unreasonableness of this demand.
Other affluent men, such as Nicodemus and Joseph of
Arimathea, wanted to follow Jesus and, indeed, became his
secret disciples, but the Gospels do not suggest that he told
them to give all their money away. Why did the Master single
out this one person, this upright and attractive young man,
and require of him such drastic sacrifice?

It is another example of the intensely *personal* character
of our Lord's ministry to individuals. Christ came as the
Physician of men's souls and he did not prescribe the same
remedy for every patient. Each case he diagnosed differently
and for each he prescribed the exact and appropriate cure. In

this case the patient needed more than medicine; he needed a surgical operation, the excision of his wealth. Some people ought to retain their wealth because, having committed themselves to Christ, they make it a powerful instrument of blessing in his hands. With the Rich Young Ruler, however, money would never be a blessing but a curse. It would always act like a malignancy on the living tissues of his soul. Therefore, it must be radically cut away, else commitment to Christ would simply soothe the pains of his restlessness; it would not remove the cause of those pains by giving him health and wholeness of personality.

We must try to understand how this drastic remedy applies to our own situation. Jesus did not prescribe poverty as a universal requisite of eternal life, but there is a larger sense in which drastic surgery may be required. On another occasion Jesus spoke of it: "And if your hand causes you to sin, cut it off; it is better for you to enter life maimed than with two hands to go to hell . . . And if your foot causes you to sin, cut it off; it is better for you to enter life lame than with two feet to be thrown into hell. And if your eye causes you to sin, pluck it out; it is better for you to enter the Kingdom of God with one eye than with two eyes to be thrown into hell."

This was Christ's own way of asserting the total sovereignty of God over human life. It was really a reiteration of the first Commandment: "Thou shalt have no other gods before me." God brooks no rival in a man's life; if there be such a rival it must not be suppressed but drastically excised with the sharp scalpel of renunciation. It may be an immoral habit, an unwholesome self-indulgence which a man excuses on the grounds that he has a right to a bit of fun now and then. It may be an attitude of mind, some prejudice or temper which he rationalizes by saying, "I can't be a Christian all the time." It may be a relationship, mean and debasing, which he secretly enjoys too much to break. Or, as in the case of the Rich Young Ruler, it may be his bank account. Look again at

George Frederick Watts' portrayal of this man. The dominant feature is the hand, a large, live, passionate hand, the fingers spread like talons, indicating a grasping, acquisitive nature that would never relax its grip on material possessions. Jesus saw no inherent evil in material possessions but instinctively he knew that this man loved them too much. Material wealth was his god. As long as he hung on to it he would always give it the first claim on his time, his thought, his energy, his devotion. It would always stand between him and the God of heaven. Therefore, if he wanted the life of the God of heaven, the full, vibrant, useful life which alone could satisfy his restless longings, he must make a choice and part with his wealth in one drastic gesture of sacrificial generosity. It was not for the sake of the poor that Jesus made this radical demand but for the sake of the young man himself. "You lack one thing," said Jesus; "go, sell what you have, and give to the poor, and you will have treasure in heaven, and come, follow me."

Blondin, the famous tight-rope walker, once balanced himself across a thin wire high above Niagara Falls while hundreds of gaping spectators held their breaths. When the incredible feat was accomplished and the applause had died down, Blondin called out, "Now, do you believe in me?" A tremendous roar of assent went up from the crowd. "All right," shouted Blondin, "who will sit on my shoulders as I make the return trip?" Deathly silence! They didn't believe in him that much.

Nor did the Rich Young Ruler believe in Jesus that much. The Master had confronted him with a basic and essential question: "How much do you really want this quality of life that you see in me? Do you want it enough to take a bold venture of faith and go out into the future stripped of everything that you hold dear?" The man had to answer, "Yes, I want eternal life, but I don't want it that much." "And he went away sorrowful," says the Gospel writer, "for he had great possessions." Such a contrast to the manner of his initial approach. He runs up to Jesus all aglow with excitement, then trudges away slowly and sorrowfully.

And Jesus let him go. That was so characteristic of the Master, so typical of his transparently honest dealings with men. Here again the modern Church has weakened itself by its refusal to learn from Jesus. One commentator speculates on the more tactful techniques by which *we* should have handled this affluent candidate for discipleship. Never would we have been so vulgar as to ask him outright for a sizeable chunk of his wealth. Our strategy would have been to get him inside the church first, make him a member of the Board, put him on the finance committee and then hope that as he sees the need he will take the hint. That is how *we* go about winning disciples for Christ. We hoodwink them. We pretend Christianity to be what it is not—a comfortable and pleasant way of life that offers everything and makes no stringent demands, a Christianity minus the Cross. Contrast the candour of our Lord's approach. Jesus never offered bargains, never concealed the Cross, never hid his scars to win a disciple. Sometimes he lost his man but he did not lose his Gospel.

So the Rich Young Ruler went away sorrowful. We can believe that Jesus shared his sorrow and felt in his own heart a genuine grief over the choice which the young man had made. The Gospel tells us that "Jesus looking upon him loved him", a love which may well have sprung from his instinctive recognition of this man's innate possibilities. What a superb disciple he might have become! What strength he might have infused into the Church! What a name he might have made for himself had he walked with Jesus and the Apostles into history! Instead, closing his relaxed fingers like a vice, he trudged sorrowfully back into anonymity. That is why Watts in his painting does not show us the man's face. It recalls a famous phrase of Dante—"One who through cowardice made the great refusal." In Dante's Hell not a single sinner in the Circle of the Avaricious can be identified. All of them are nameless, faceless. The man who values possessions above personality finds his Nemesis in the ultimate loss of his own personality. For a few acres of land and a few bags of gold he surrenders everything that could make him a person, a child of God through all eternity.

That was the tragedy of the Rich Young Ruler, and it is the tragedy of many people today. In their search for happiness, contentment and adventure they turn in every direction except the direction of Christ. How infinitely poorer the Church is without them! Yet it is not the Church but they who are the real losers; for in refusing the demands that Christ makes of them, they refuse also the gift that he offers— the gift of eternal life.

CHAPTER XII

WITH FOUR FISHERMEN

At a church in St. Leonards-on-Sea there is a most unusual pulpit. It resembles the prow of a Galilean fishing boat. It is an authentic piece of craftsmanship because it was constructed by modern Israeli fishermen of the Ein Gev Kibbutz on the eastern shore of the Sea of Galilee. Whoever proclaims the Gospel from this pulpit will surely know that he stands securely on the historical fact out of which the Gospel was born. He will also be humbled by the awareness of his identification with the historic Jesus.

One incident will always be uppermost in the preacher's mind, the incident recorded in the fifth chapter of Luke's Gospel which tells of a day when Jesus did, in fact, proclaim the good news from such a pulpit. A huge crowd had assembled at the sea-shore to hear from his lips the word of life. Closer and closer the people pressed until, stepping back to make room for them, Jesus felt the shallow water encircling his ankles. He noticed some boats drawn up on the beach. It was early morning, and after a night's fishing the owners were washing their nets. Beckoning to one of these men, a big, burly fisherman named Simon, Jesus asked a favour which Simon readily granted. Together they climbed into the boat, pushed out a few yards from the land and dropped anchor. Then, standing in the prow, Jesus faced his congregation and began to preach.

It would be an unforgettable scene, so easily etched in our minds—the boat in the foreground, Jesus with his back to us; in front of him, listening intently, the eager crowd covering the beach and the grassy bank; behind them the green vineyards and fields of olive trees; and in the background the Mount of Beatitudes capped by a brilliant blue sky.

Luke does not tell us what Jesus said in his sermon from Simon's boat. Instead, he describes in vivid detail the incident that followed. He has good reason to do so, because this incident, which took place on the shore of an obscure lake, changed the course of history. Before Jesus preached that day from his unconventional pulpit there was not and there never had been another Christian in the whole world. His call to the four fishermen to forsake their nets and become fishers of men marked in a very real sense the birth of the Christian Church, the beginning of that long procession of apostles, saints, martyrs, missionaries and reformers that stretches down the centuries and encircles the globe.

The response of these men not only changed the course of history; it changed the course of their own lives. This was their crucial encounter with Jesus. Like every encounter in our Lord's personal ministry it follows a pattern which has been repeated and may still be repeated wherever men encounter the living Christ of God.

It begins with something that Jesus did—*a Divine act of grace and power*. After the crowds had dispersed Jesus noticed for the first time that there were no fish in the boat. Turning to Simon, he said, "Put out into the deep and let down your nets for a catch." We can imagine the amused thoughts in Simon's mind, "Who but an amateur would suggest such a foolish idea? If the fish don't bite at night they certainly don't bite in the daytime." "Master," he replied patiently, "we toiled all night and took nothing." Yet, to humour Jesus, perhaps, or because the Master's manner compelled him, he added, "But at your word I will let down the nets." No doubt the other fishermen standing on the shore laughed at the sight of Simon trying his luck after a profitless night, a laughter that quickly turned to gaping astonishment as Simon suddenly shouted across the water, "Come out quickly. I need your help! My net is breaking with fish!" What happened after that must surely have become the biggest fish story ever told in the region of Capernaum, because in the end the catch was so great that it loaded two boats to the point of sinking.

Not that the phenomenal catch necessarily seemed miraculous to the fishermen. In the Sea of Galilee it was not unusual even in the daytime for a solid shoal of fish to appear near the surface of the water, and they would assume that Jesus with his keen eye had seen such a shoal. It was not the fish that impressed them but the awareness that Jesus had touched their lives in a new and decisive way. Everything about the incident suggests that they had seen him many times before, had conversed with him, felt the magnetism of his personality, listened to his teachings and witnessed some of his mighty acts. Yet somehow he had never really gotten through to them until this day when he used their boat as a pulpit and moved into their situation with an act of grace and power.

We must read this story as a microcosm of the Gospel, because the first moment in the whole drama of redemption is the act whereby God takes the initiative and moves into our human situation with Divine grace and power. Some world religions begin with man himself, man in his quest for truth, man searching for God by way of reasoned argument and mystic contemplation. Christians themselves often mistakenly start at this point. They set out to prove the existence of God, they read books and hold discussions about him; they construct, as it were, a ladder ascending from earth to heaven. In so doing they ignore the historical basis of Christianity which is not something that we do but something that God does, a ladder fastened at the top whereby God himself takes the initiative and descends into our situation with a Divine act of grace and power.

What is that act? Historically an event—the life, death and resurrection of a man named Jesus of Nazareth. As an event it happened at a particular time in history and at a particular place on the earth's surface but, like all events, it is inseparable from its impact upon those who witnessed it. Without their witness, writes Emil Brunner, the story of Jesus "would have echoed and re-echoed like a sound which passes unheard in a primeval forest". What was their witness? That Jesus of Nazareth was different from other men. Like Socrates he taught Divine truth, but unlike Socrates he taught and incarnated in his own person the truth of self-negating love. Like Socrates he died a martyr's death, but unlike Socrates he broke the power of death because, after his crucified body had been sealed in a rock-hewn tomb, he appeared again to his followers, alive. To the men who witnessed it, and whose witness is recorded in the New Testament, this Christ-event allowed of only one explanation—God dwelt in it, God himself taking the initiative and moving into our human situation with a Divine act of grace and power.

So we come to the second moment in our crucial encounter —*man's recoil from this Divine act of grace and power*. We should expect Simon Peter and the other fishermen to be overjoyed by this sudden stroke of good fortune after a long night's fruitless toil. Apparently, however, the "miracle" did not have that effect upon them at all. Quite the opposite, in fact. Recovering from his initial astonishment, Simon Peter fell down at Jesus' knees and cried out, "Depart from me, for I am a sinful man, O Lord!" Peter had seen Jesus before but only through clouded human eyes. In this moment he saw him clearly through the eyes of faith, and what Peter saw blinded him, judged him and lighted up the poverty and tawdriness of his own soul.

We can find a parallel in our own experience. Who among us has not felt humbled by the presence of a personality stronger, cleaner and nobler than himself? We thought we were doing well enough morally until we became aware of the difference between his life and ours. We saw him rise with calm courage to a crisis which threw us into panic. We saw him perform deeds of sacrifice far beyond the range of our narrow self-interest. Then for the first time we began to see ourselves; and the whole idea of sin ceased to be a pious prayer-phrase and became an acute and personal disquiet. Towards such a person we have mingled feelings. He attracts us and he disturbs us. We want to be with him, yet we also want to get as far away from him as possible.

"Depart from me, for I am a sinful man, O Lord." In what tone of voice did Peter utter that cry of poignant contrition? Did he speak harshly? "Depart from me! Go away! Now that I know who you are I want nothing to do with you. I like my sin, my alcoholism, my adultery, my bad-temperedness and my pride. I have learned to live with it and I don't want you around making me feel guilty!" Or did he speak in a tone of wistful regret? "Depart from me!" But then, he would have called himself an "old sinner". That's how the retort usually comes. "Don't bother with me, padre, I'm not worth it. I'm past being saved. There was a time, once, in my youth. But it's too late now. Go away and preach your Gospel to someone else." Was that how Peter spoke or was it in a voice of agony that came from the depths of his soul? "Depart from me, for I am a sinful man, O Lord! How can I be where you are, the Holy One of God? How can you and I inhabit the same order of reality? How can I, sinner that I am, stand in the presence of the Most High?"

Peter's cry alone? No, the cry of every man who really encounters Christ and knows himself judged by the blinding vision of God's holiness in Christ. I used to wonder why some people refuse to darken the door of a church and for a time I even believed their profession of intellectual doubts and took seriously their criticisms of Christianity's irrelevance. Now I can see through the smokescreen of their inverted piety. They *want* to doubt, they *want* to believe Christianity irrelevant, they *want* to stand outside the Church, because it means that nothing need disturb the green scum which has settled on the stagnant surface of their souls. Outside the

Church they can lead unexamined lives. Inside the Church, confronted by the glorious manhood of Christ, they will know that they have sinned and fallen far short of that glory; and seeing that it cost God the Cross to forgive them, they will realize the depth and enormity of their sin. Easier, then, to remain outside. It is their way, and sometimes our way, of saying to Jesus, "Depart from me, for I am a sinful man, O Lord!"

But it makes the third moment in our crucial encounter all the more wonderful, for this is *the moment of Christ's acceptance.* Look at the very human Peter on his knees in the tossing boat, his head between his hands, his big body racked with sobs as he knows himself judged by the holiness of God in Christ. Suddenly he looks up, expecting to see sternness and censure in the Master's eyes. Instead, to his amazement, he sees there an expression of tender, forgiving love. Jesus smiles. "Do not be afraid," he assures the fishermen, "henceforth you will be catching men."

Jesus did not depart from Peter, though he knew Peter better than the man knew himself. Nor did he say, "Yes you are a sinful man. But you have admitted it now, so there is some hope for you. Take hold of yourself. Reform your conduct. Try to lead a better life, and one of these days we shall talk the whole matter over again." That alone were grace beyond our deserving—that God should not cast us off but should forgive our sins and allow us another chance to rebuild the character we have wrecked. God does something infinitely more marvellous than that, however. He accepts us in the midst of our sin and in spite of our sin. He makes no stipulations, lays down no conditions, asks nothing save the admission of our unworthiness and our need of his grace.

Look more closely at these Galilean fishermen. Here was Simon Peter, a rough sort of man who had never known anything but the rough life of the fishing fleet. He might well confess his weakness because one day, in spite of his hot impulses and boastful manner, he would tempt Jesus to deflect from the will of God; in the hour of crisis he would turn coward and deny his Master shamefully. Look at James and his brother John, a pair of hot-heads, well nicknamed "Sons of Thunder", who would want to call down fire from heaven on a village that rejected Jesus; ambitious, self-seeking men who would ask for the places of honour at his right hand in the Kingdom of God.* The Church has since canonized these disciples, turned them into "saints", but they don't seem a very saintly lot when we meet them on the shores of the Sea of Galilee or even months later in a Jerusalem Upper Room. Yet to such men as these, not as they might one day by the grace of God become, but even as they were now in all their human frailty and unworthiness, God's Messiah committed the issues of his Kingdom. "Do not be afraid," he said, "henceforth you will be catching men."

Look at the fishermen; then look at yourself. Do so and you will realize how truly wonderful is this third moment in your crucial encounter with Christ. Not only does he accept you but he calls you to follow him and become his disciple and share in his mighty work of redemption. We had better ponder this fact. To us, not to some non-existent super-race of spiritual giants, the Master's challenge still comes, "Henceforth you will be catching men." Christians might well afford to study the implications of that metaphor in their techniques of commending the Faith to unbelievers. A wise friend of mine used to say that every minister of the Gospel ought to take up fishing, because it would teach him the lesson of patience. He would not be disheartened by long nights of fruitless toil nor would he be surprised by the appearance of sudden shoals when the power of Christ fills his net to the point of breaking. We are the fishermen. It is at once sober-ing and exhilarating to realize that Christ has entrusted to us

* The briefer accounts of this incident in the Gospels of Matthew and Mark indicate that Peter's brother, Andrew, was among those whom Jesus called that day.

the future of his ministry upon earth. Not as we might one day by his grace become, but even as we are now in all our unworthiness and frailty, Christ accepts us and commits to us the issues of his Kingdom in our generation.

That brings us to the final moment in this crucial encounter by the Sea of Galilee—*the act of sacrificial surrender.* The Gospel writer simply tells us that when the four fishermen had brought their boats to land, "they left everything and followed him." Such a contrast to the Rich Young Ruler who also encountered Jesus but "turned away sorrowful, because he had great possessions"! He made the great refusal; the four fishermen made the great acceptance. It might be argued that in terms of material goods they had not so much to lose, but what more can a man lose than his property, his means of livelihood, his home, his security? All of these things the fishermen surrendered in answer to the call of Christ. "They left everything"; and it doesn't matter whether that "everything" is an inherited fortune or a fishing boat and a few nets. What does matter is that Jesus invited them to a great venture of faith, a perilous pilgrimage into the unknown, and they accepted. They said "Yes" to Christ.

That is what it means to be a Christian. At no point in the New Testament and certainly at no point in the personal ministry of Jesus do you find our religion set forth as a full-blown theological system which must be accepted in its entirety or not at all. One young person will say, "I feel attracted to Jesus but I shall not become a Christian, because there are still too many beliefs such as the Trinity and the Virgin Birth and the physical Resurrection, which I do not understand." We can only reply that neither did the disciples understand these things or very much else on the day they left everything and followed Jesus. They didn't even understand Jesus himself. All they knew was that he had brought within their experience the love and power and holiness and judgment and forgiveness of God and that more than anything else in the world they wanted to be with him. That is all that any of us can expect in our first crucial encounter with God's Christ. Christ increases our knowledge, but only as we act on the basis of the knowledge which he has already given us. That is Christian discipleship, that and nothing more—an act of sacrificial surrender whereby we say "Yes" to Christ.

The more I ponder on what it means to be a Christian, the more I realize that on our side it reduces itself to simple obedience. We can ask no guarantees of God, make no bargains with him. People who want everything proved to their intellectual satisfaction before taking the plunge of faith are going to stand on the edge of the pool for the rest of their lives. So are the people who want some mystical experience, some supernatural voice or vision or some inner intoxication that can as easily be induced by the contents of a bottle. J. H. Oldham writes, "There are some things in life—and they may be the most important things—that we cannot know by research or reflection, but only by committing ourselves. We must dare in order to know." Certainly that truth applies to marriage. The couple who keep postponing their wedding until they feel absolutely sure of each other will have nothing to look forward to but a very long engagement. It is even more true of Christian discipleship. In Jesus God touches our lives with a Divine act of grace and power. Unworthy as we are, God accepts us and calls us. And nothing more happens until we say "Yes" to Christ and follow him.

Because the four fishermen did accept what the Rich Young Ruler refused they also gained all that the Rich Young Ruler and many others missed. They gained a great friendship, a love that never let them go and in the end re-made them in its own image. They gained a great development, an evolution of character that took them from their common trade into universal sainthood. They gained a great adventure, leading roles in the most decisive drama ever played, an enduring place in history. All of these Christ still offers as he encounters us through the Church's ministry and sacraments, through the Bible, through a Christlike personality or through some other more silent and hidden way. Still he invites us to make the great acceptance. Still he calls us to say "Yes".

CHAPTER XIII

WITH A DYING CRIMINAL

ONE bit-player in the Good Friday drama has always fascinated me—the Penitent Thief who was crucified with Jesus and to whom the dying Saviour granted the promise of paradise. Tradition gives him the name of Dismas, but we cannot be certain of his name nor do we know anything definite about his background. We only know that he played a supporting role on the stage of Calvary and, therefore, upon the stage of history. He has the distinction of being the last man alive to benefit by the personal ministry of the earthly Jesus. Whenever I read the story of the Crucifixion in the twenty-third chapter of Luke's Gospel I look at this Penitent Thief, at his crucial encounter with God's Christ, and I ask the same questions about him.

What prompted his radical change of heart? The Gospels suggest that, like his henchman on the other cross, he was a hardened criminal who had been sentenced for the most heinous crimes. Therefore he must have been a tough character, determined to die as defiantly as he had lived. Yet on the cross he not only rebuked his partner for jeering at Jesus but actually sprang to our Lord's defence and pleaded for the mercy of heaven. Why? How shall we account for it?

The answer suggests itself. What happened to this man in the eleventh hour was the very thing which had happened to sinful men and women all through the Gospel story, people like Simon Peter and Zacchaeus and Mary Magdalene and the woman of Samaria, who came under the influence of Jesus and felt his transforming power. What happened to the Penitent Thief is the very thing which happens now to every man who comes to the Cross and looks into the face of the dying Saviour. Against the white background of the crucified Lord the blackness of his own character stands revealed; yet, though the Cross judges him, he reaches out to it as his one hope of forgiveness and redemption. The Penitent Thief may have been the last man to speak with the earthly Jesus but he was the first among millions to feel the saving impact of the Cross.

Can we put ourselves in his place and try to imagine the thoughts that churned in his mind as he carried his cross in the dreadful procession to Golgotha? "Crucified by the filthy Romans! What a way to die! Well, we bargained for it. We haven't lived like cowards and we are not going to die like cowards . . ." One thing puzzles the prisoner. He can't figure out the third member of the party, Jesus of Nazareth, the one whom the crowd is jeering at. "He looks too meek to commit a crime, can't even stand up under the weight of his own cross. They're getting someone to carry it for him." As the morning sun beats down relentlessly, however, even our bold thief feels his own knees buckling and he looks with envy on Jesus, now walking upright. Then a wave of pity surges through him. "Poor devil! No wonder he's weak. They've been scourging him. See his back, all raw and bloody. Yes, you Romans, you're very brave when you've got a whip in your hands. I wish to God I had a whip . . ."

They come to a skull-shaped hill outside the city wall— Golgotha, the place of execution. This is the end of the road for all of them. Tough as they are, the condemned thief and his henchman gulp down the wine mixed with myrrh, the sedative to deaden the pain. Only a fool would refuse it. "What, then, is this other fellow, the one who won't drink the drug—a fool, or . . . what? He'll be sorry." In a moment the awful work begins, the work of nailing hands and feet to instruments of torture. There is a crunching of bone and a searing pain as the blood begins to flow freely. Up go the crosses, and in moves the mocking mob screaming like blood-thirsty animals. The thieves spit at them, "Dirty, stinking, rotten hypocrites. Every one of them would be hanging here if the Romans could read their thoughts . . ."

Suddenly the thief sees that they are not mocking him at all. It's the man on the centre cross, Jesus of Nazareth. He's the underdog. "Yell back at them, Jesus . . . Don't take it from the filthy . . ." Our thief stops short. "The face of the man! He doesn't look angry with the crowd. There's no hatred in his eyes . . . only sorrow and pity. His lips are moving 'Father . . . forgive . . . them . . . for . . . they . . . know . . . not . . . what . . . they . . . do!' Know not what they do? How stupid can you get? It's him that doesn't know what he is doing—asking God to forgive such ignorance and cruelty!"

A familiar voice rises above the shrieking mob "If thou be Christ, save thyself and us!" Our thief can hardly believe his ears. It is the voice of his henchman, his partner in crime. "What does he think he's doing . . . trying to curry favour with the crowd, get a last-minute reprieve or something by cursing this poor, defenceless wretch hanging between us? You only have to look at him to see that he's no criminal like we are." Every word an agony, our thief bursts out, "Hold your tongue, you fool. Don't you fear the wrath of God? We're all in this together—you and I for good reason. We're only getting what we deserve. But can't you see that this man is innocent? He hasn't done anything wrong. He has suffered enough. For God's sake leave him alone!" Jesus turns and looks at the thief.

Such a look! It shakes our criminal to the very depths, throwing his drunken thoughts into complete chaos. He sees gratitude in those eyes, yet they burn into his soul, judging him, condemning him. "He knows me. I have never seen him before but I'll swear he knows everything about me, every dirty corner of my life . . . But he isn't angry. He's sorry for me. He understands . . . My father used to look at me in that

way. He loved me no matter what I did, loved me and forgave me . . . I want Jesus to forgive me. I don't know why.
Maybe it's because he is here, on the Cross, beside me. He
hasn't done any wrong but he's being punished like I am,
suffering like I am . . . He knows. He understands." His eyes
about to close for ever, the dying thief gasps, "Jesus, Lord, I
don't know who you are but I have watched you die and I
know that the Cross won't be the end of you. Soon you'll
be done with it and you'll be with God in your Kingdom. I
am sorry for what I have been. Will you forgive me? Will you
remember me when you come into your kingdom . . .?"

Does that explain, even partly, the eleventh-hour repentance
of this dying criminal? Can we not say with assurance that
he was the first man in history to experience the saving power
of the Cross? That is where the Gospel begins. It does not
begin with some acceptable image of God, as certain theologians contend. The dying thief *had* no image of God. He
didn't know what God is like nor did he care. All he knew
was that the man hanging beside him in death represented
the cleanest, strongest, tenderest embodiment of manhood that
he had ever seen and that, if he had any link with eternity at
all, any claim on the clemency of heaven, it was through the
compassion of this Man. Nor does the Gospel begin with a
sordid sense of our own sin, because apart from the sight of
what it cost God to forgive our sins we have no idea how sordid our sins really are. Read the New Testament, especially
the letters of Paul, if you want to know where the Gospel
begins. Before ever theorizing about God or stirring within
us a sense of guilt, Paul takes us to a Cross where the great,
loving heart of God is laid bare to the whole world and where,
knowing ourselves judged and condemned, we cry out from
the depths of our human need, "Jesus, Lord, remember me
when thou comest into thy kingdom."

Jesus answered the Penitent Thief's prayer. He granted
him a boon beyond all expectation, a word of forgiveness that

wiped the slate clean, cancelled his crimes and gave him a blessed hope of heaven. "Verily I say unto thee, today thou shalt be with me in paradise."

That raises a second question about this crucial encounter on Calvary, a question such as that asked by the labourers in the vineyard when they saw that those who had worked only one hour received exactly the same wage as those who had toiled all day. We ask, *How could Jesus forgive this dying criminal?* Would it not have been more just if he had refused the request and said, "No, my friend. It's too late for repentance. You've had your chance with life and failed. So now you can suffer the consequences." Is it right that a man should go through his whole life cursing God and destroying his fellow-men and with a single pious word on his death-bed secure acquittal before the bar of heaven? Remorseful or scared as this thief may have been on the cross, how could Jesus possibly forgive him for the kind of life that he had lived?

We shall find the answer by setting this incident in the light of the total ministry of Jesus. Whenever Jesus encountered a sinner he judged that person not by what he had done but what he was. With his X-ray vision he peered into the inner recesses of the human soul. Even on Calvary, almost blinded by the pains of death, he nevertheless knew what manner of man it was who hung at his side—not a hardened cynic but a disillusioned idealist, not a man of evil purpose but a victim of cruel circumstance. The mob looked at the tough face of this criminal and saw only the ignoble end of his life. Jesus looked behind that face and saw the essential direction of his life.

It has been suggested that the Penitent Thief had something in common with Jesus. Originally he served the same purpose but resorted to a different means of achieving it. Let us try to reconstruct his story. As a boy he was probably brought up in a God-fearing Jewish home, guided by wise and loving parents, educated in the sacred writings of his people. Throughout these writings one theme beat relentlessly on his brain—the hope of a Messiah, God's representative, who would come as a mighty conqueror to establish a new world Kingdom with Jerusalem as its capital. That was Israel's hope, and increasingly he made it his hope. Perhaps, as he grew older, he became a Zealot, focusing his life towards one consuming purpose—to free his people from the iron yoke of Rome and make ready for the promised Kingdom of the Messiah.

At first he tried to keep within the law, moving among his friends, imparting his enthusiasm and arguing passionately like a political agitator. As apathy and conservatism blocked his path, however, he began to despair of gaining his ends by legitimate means. Unable to stir up his people into open rebellion, he organized a guerrilla band, skulking in the mountains and swooping down to attack small detachments of Roman soldiers. That would give them a foretaste of their punishment in the Messianic Kingdom! Even guerrilla soldiers must eat, so, pressured by hunger, he and his men began infesting the trade routes and robbing wealthy caravans. One day their victims resisted, and blood-letting became a necessity. He had never dreamed of this and recoiled from it at first, but it continued to happen until he became brutal and callous, even to the point of murder. When we meet him carrying his cross to Calvary, he is no clean and ardent patriot but a disgraced and hardened criminal.

If this were his story, we cannot explain his cry from the cross as a mere death-bed repentance. What actually happened, I believe, was that the sight of Jesus dying beside him fanned into flame the smouldering fire of his early idealism. Suddenly on the threshold of death he saw the catastrophic mistake of his life. He saw that the Kingdom of Heaven is not a political kingdom of earthly power and glory but a spiritual Kingdom of heavenly love and peace and goodness. He saw also that the way to that Kingdom goes not through violent revolution and war but through humble service and suffering. It may also be that he recognized in the man who hung beside him the very King whose coming he had long awaited. Not some military conqueror but this crucified friend of sinners was Israel's Messiah. All that our thief had worked and struggled and killed for, Jesus was now going to inherit by dying. Like the Prodigal Son in the parable, the Penitent Thief in real life "came to himself". His cry "Jesus, Lord, remember me when thou comest into thy Kingdom," expressed not so much a radical change of heart as a reassertion of the innermost purpose of his life. Jesus saw that and on that basis judged him.

A medieval monk said that everyone who gets to heaven will be surprised by three things. First he will be surprised to see many he did not think would be there. Second he will be surprised that some are not there whom he expected to see. Third he will be surprised that he himself is there. C. S. Lewis made this the theme of his satirical book, *The Great Divorce*.* It is the story of a bus-load of ghosts who travel from hell to heaven just to visit the place and see if they would like to remain there permanently. What utterly astonishes them is to find among the citizens of heaven people who on earth were downright immoral and unreligious—adulterers, heretics and murderers. When the visitors ask the reason for this strange reversal of human justice, the answer they receive is that God's judgments differ from man's. The God who revealed himself in Christ bases his verdict not on the outward conduct of life but on the inner intention of the heart.

Remember that truth when your sense of moral failure plunges you into a pit of self-loathing; remember it when society censures you and your friends turn their backs in scorn. Remember that God looks not at what you have done but at what you are; he looks inside your soul to the intention of your heart and the direction of your life. God sees everything about you, the best as well as the worst. He sees all those flickering impulses of genuine compassion which you have felt

* Geoffrey Bles, London, 1946.

towards other people but which you were too awkward to communicate to them. He sees the decent motives which have gone out from you in a fairly straightforward fashion but have somehow become all twisted and misunderstood amid the confusing web of human relationships. He sees that inner core of sensitivity and humility and hope which lies buried beneath the protective shell of your personality. God knows that deep inside you are the makings of a better person than you have ever been, and on the basis of these he forms his final judgment.

One further question about the Penitent Thief: *What did his repentance matter?* What good did a radical change of heart and a pardoning word from Jesus do him in the eleventh hour? His life was about to end. To be sure, he could now die peacefully, but is that so very important?

No, it is not important if you believe that death is really the end and if you agree with Bertrand Russell who said, "I believe that when I die I shall rot, and nothing of my ego will survive." But suppose death is not the end? Suppose Jesus spoke the truth when he said that there are many mansions in the Father's house, and suppose Paul spoke the truth when he said, "We must all appear before the judgment seat of Christ, so that each one may receive good or evil, according to what he has done in the body"? Then it means that our moral struggle does not end with the grave but continues beyond the grave. When this earthly, visible chapter of life closes, life moves on to new chapters, new tasks and relationships, new disciplines and opportunities. It means that God himself does not have to pay his accounts at the end of each week; God has all eternity in which to judge, chasten and perfect us and fulfil his purpose for our lives.

It was really not a very large favour that this dying criminal asked of Jesus, "Remember me when thou comest into thy Kingdom . . . don't forget that I stood up for you . . . Say a good word for me to the great Judge upon his throne";

F

not a large favour but it bespoke a large faith that when *he* was done with his cross he, too, might find himself before the great Judge upon his throne. And Jesus granted him a boon beyond expectation—not a mere promise, "Yes, I shall remember you," but a triumphant assurance, "Today . . . this very day . . . thou shalt be with me in paradise."

That is all any of us have a right to expect at the end of life's journey and that is all we know with any certainty about paradise. In a Roman prison cell the Apostle Paul, having loved and served Christ since the day he encountered him on the Damascus Road, looked into the face of execution without fear because he knew that, whatever happened to him, he couldn't lose anyway. To live longer meant Christ; to die meant more of Christ. When you love a person with your whole heart, the only thing in life you really want is to be with that person for ever, because only in his presence are you really and truly alive. To live eternally with our beloved Christ—that is the Christian hope of paradise.

Christ gave that hope to a dying criminal who presumably did *not* love him and who, perhaps, had fought against everything that he stood for. It was more than a hope that Christ gave; it was a promise, an assurance, a guarantee and therefore the most momentous thing that happened on Black Friday. "Today thou shalt be with me in paradise." That one word spoken from the Cross makes the Crucifixion intensely personal for so many people. It takes the Calvary drama out of the liturgical stratosphere, sweeps away the aura of gloom and piety and brings it into direct contact with real life. What Christ on his Cross said to the condemned criminal who hung beside him he still says to every convict, every murderer, every whore, every dope-fiend, every depraved, degraded wreck of a human being. The Penitent Thief is the patron saint of all "poor devils". Such people the living Christ still encounters and tells them that no sin is greater than his grace and no hour in life too late to turn to him.

I once read of a beautiful act of priestly absolution that was performed by a nurse in a hospital. They brought in from the ambulance a young woman who had been stabbed in a drunken brawl in a disreputable district of the city. She was dying, and the doctor asked the nurse to sit by the unconscious girl until death came. As the nurse looked at her, thinking what a pity it was that a face so young should have such coarse lines on it, the girl opened her eyes. "I want you to tell me something and tell me straight," she said. "Do you think God cares about people like me? Do you think he could forgive anyone as bad as me?"

The nurse dared not answer at first, not until she had breathed a prayer and taken the girl's hand as though to feel at one with her. Then, knowing it to be true, she answered "I'm telling you straight: God cares about you and he forgives you." The girl gave a little sigh and slipped back into unconsciousness, the lines on her face changing as death approached. "I believe," said the man who wrote about this incident, "that something momentous happened between God and that girl through the nurse and that it had something to do with what happened long ago on a certain 'green hill far away, without a city wall'."

CHAPTER XIV

WITH A DESPONDENT PAIR

ONE group of people puzzles me. Those are the stated-occasion Christians who every spring come to life with the blossoms and at Easter pay their annual visit to church. Not that I am critical of them. I feel sorry for what they have missed. How can they get anything more from the Christian drama than a theatre-goer who slips into his reserved seat only for the last act of a play? How can they rejoice in the risen Christ unless they have walked with the human Jesus and sorrowed over his death upon the Cross?

This is indeed the joy of Easter—the breathtaking good news that he who was crucified, dead and buried has burst the bonds of death and is alive for evermore. His personal ministry of teaching and healing and redemption, begun in the days of his flesh, has not stopped; it has been released from the restrictions of time and space and set free to operate with power throughout the world. The same Jesus, who encountered those who needed him on the roads of Galilee and Judea, still encounters us as we need him on the road of life. All that the human Jesus did for men and women in ancient Palestine the risen Christ does for us now when we consciously open our lives in faith to receive him.

We have seen our own likeness in many of the people whom Jesus encountered. On the evening of Easter Day we recognize ourselves in a pair of despondent disciples who trudge their weary way home from Jerusalem to Emmaus. Christ is risen and is abroad in a springtime world, but Cleopas and his companion do not know it. They have no picture in their minds but that of the Cross and the sealed tomb. Their shoulders are slumped and their heads downcast, as though they bear on their backs a crushing burden of dejection and disillusionment. Even when the risen Christ catches up with them and walks beside them, their eyes are so blinded by grief that they do not recognize him. These two men are really depressed, down in the dumps, "full of gloom", as the *New English Bible* describes their condition.

We can identify ourselves with them easily enough. Though we may not suffer from some of the maladies that Jesus cured during the course of his healing ministry, we do know what it is to feel depressed. Most of us have days when all the joy seems to have gone out of life, when the whole world appears blue, and we feel so melancholy that any enforced heartiness on the part of other people only jars our nerves. Usually we can associate low spirits with low physical vitality, such as the exhaustion that a preacher suffers on Monday mornings. Years ago a wise colleague warned me never to make an important decision on Mondays. More often the feeling of despondency comes upon us unawares like a common cold, and no matter how we doctor ourselves we cannot hasten our recovery. We just have to let depression take its course.

It is utterly superficial to say that if a man were really a believing Christian he would always be cheerful and never depressed. Some of the saintliest men in history, men who brought great courage and cheer to others, were themselves subject to fits of depression. The Bible makes no guarantee that we shall not fall into the slough of despond but it does introduce us to One who rescues us from the slough of despond. This is the good news of Easter, the joyous truth that the risen Christ, who encountered the despondent pair on the Emmaus Road, encounters us and does for us what he did for them.

He isolated the cause of their despondency. We can believe that for a while, as Christ walked beside them, he said nothing. Perhaps they were too busy communicating their mutual misery even to notice him. Suddenly he broke in and asked, "What is this conversation which you are holding with each other as you walk?" Luke, who records this encounter at some length in the twenty-fourth chapter of his Gospel, describes their reaction: "And they stood still, looking sad."

That might be a good thing to do when you feel depressed —stand still, stop talking and ask yourself, "Why are my spirits so low?" It is not always possible to isolate the cause. Depression, especially if it occurs frequently and lasts a long time, may have its source in a psychopathic condition far below the surface of the conscious mind; in which case the answer lies not in religion but in specialized medical treatment. As a young minister I made frequent visits to a woman who suffered prolonged fits of melancholy and I innocently tried to cheer her up. It was like telling a man with a rope around his neck to sing Psalms. Unhappily no-one succeeded in removing the rope from this poor woman's neck, and eventually she took her own life.

From boyhood Abraham Lincoln suffered severe spells of melancholy, but after the tragic death of his fiancée, Ann Rutledge, they became more frequent and sometimes verged almost upon insanity. Once he confessed to a friend that although he seemed to others to enjoy life rapturously yet when alone he was so overcome by mental depression that he did not dare to carry a pocket-knife. Before his wedding to Mary Todd he was found wandering about in such a depressed state that he had to be watched day and night for fear that he might do something desperate. Weeks later he wrote to his law partner: "Whether I shall ever be better I cannot tell; I awfully forebode that I shall not. To remain as I am is impossible. I must die or be better, as it appears to me."

We are concerned, however, not with abnormal depression, but with the more normal type that can be traced to a specific cause. Our first step in dealing with it is to isolate that cause, face it frankly and, if possible, talk it over with a friend.

Christ helped Cleopas and his companion to do this. The *King James Version* translates his question: "What manner of communications are these that ye have one to another, as ye walk, and are sad?" So they told him about the Crucifixion of their Master. They rehearsed the dreadful details of the arrest, the trial, the scourging, the execution and the burial; and one can imagine that even this unburdening of their grief to a total stranger had its therapeutic effect, raising their spirits ever so slightly.

Sometimes the unburdening of our hearts to the God who revealed himself in Christ has an even more marked effect. Isaac Watts called prayer our means of converse with God; and true conversation involves listening as well as talking. If in our prayers we "stood still", as the disciples did, and simply listened we might hear the voice of God asking, "Well, what's troubling you? Out with it!" The miracle of such prayer is that not infrequently the mists of time evaporate in the sunlight of eternity, and we emerge from the secret place with new heart and stronger spirit. Someone has expressed it poetically:

"*Lord, what a change within us one short hour*
Spent in Thy presence will prevail to make!
What heavy burdens from our bosoms take,
What parched grounds refresh as with a shower!
We kneel, and all around us seems to lower;
We rise, and all, the distant and the near,
Stands forth in sunny outline brave and clear;
We kneel, how weak! we rise, how full of power!"*

The next thing Christ did for the two men was to show them that *their depressed mood was rooted in their own self-pity*. Concluding their grim recital about the death of Jesus,

* Richard C. Trench. Quoted in *Masterpieces of Religious Verse*, ed. by James Dalton Morrison (Harper and Brothers, New York and London, 1948).

they burst out, "But we had hoped that he was the one to redeem Israel." Ah, there it was—the true source of their misery. It was not the Crucifixion that plunged them into deepest gloom but the shattering effect of the Crucifixion upon all their hopes and dreams. They felt sorry, not only that their Messiah had been killed but that his death had deprived Israel of her restored glory. Not Jesus but they themselves held the centre of the stage in their dismal drama.

Did they, perhaps, find a morbid comfort in this self-dramatization? Occasionally one suspects that some people so enjoy feeling melancholy that they deliberately induce the mood of depression. Shakespeare's Hamlet was such a person.

> *"O that this too too solid flesh would melt,*
> *Thaw and resolve itself into a dew;*
> *Or that the Everlasting had not fix'd*
> *His canon 'gainst self-slaughter. O God! O God!*
> *How weary, stale, flat, and unprofitable*
> *Seem to me all the uses of the world."*

The melancholy Dane dramatized himself. Outwardly he mourned his father's death and deplored his mother's early betrothal to his uncle, but self-pity lay at the source of Hamlet's depression. From first to last he set himself in the centre of the stage and made his own drama one of tragedy.

Elijah tried to do the same thing. This Hebrew prophet, forsaken, despised, hunted like a beast of prey, felt so depressed that he fled into the wilderness, crawled into a cave and prayed that God would take away his life. Instead God tracked him down and asked, "What are you doing here, Elijah?" Out came the bitter complaint of Israel's apostasy and her murder of God's messengers. "I, even I only am left; and they seek my life to take it away." Did God coddle this man's self-pity? By no means. He said, in effect, "Come off it, Elijah. You can stop pretending to be solicitous for me. You know that I have the situation in hand. Go back to the work

I have given you and remove yourself from the centre of the stage!"

Whatever else it may accomplish, a crucial encounter with the God who revealed himself in Christ is bound to have this effect. Indeed, we can be with Christ on no other terms. At the height of his ministry, as he warned the disciples of his impending sacrifice, Jesus told them that, because he must walk the road of self-negating love, so they, if they wanted to follow him, must be prepared to walk that same road. "If any man would come after me, let him deny himself and take up his cross and follow me." By self-denial he did not mean the renunciation of little luxuries which some religious people associate with the season of Lent. Jesus was telling them, and us, that the way of the Cross is a way of complete self-effacement. He was telling them that the healthy, happy, well-integrated life is essentially the outgoing life, the unselfish, giving life. The man who walks with Christ does not dramatize himself because he does not think of himself. He is less concerned with what happens to him than with what he ought to be doing in obedience to the will of God. The tragedy of the world may plunge him into depression, but Christ rescues him from a sense of his own tragedy by removing him from the centre of the stage.

There is at least one class of people who rarely complain of feeling depressed. These are the servants of Christ, the missionaries and social reformers and ordinary folk who are so engrossed in the problems of others that they have no time to think about their own. I remember such a man whom I shall call Wallace Wilson. He had abundant reason to be melancholy because every evening he came home to an empty house that reminded him of his beloved wife who was an incurable patient in a mental hospital. Tirelessly he absorbed himself in community service, in the work of the Church and in the needs of the underprivileged. When people expressed admiration for his serene courage, he used to reply, "I am all right as long as I don't think about Wallace Wilson. I thank

God that he gives me so much to do for him that I haven't time to worry about myself."

Returning to the despondent pair on the Emmaus Road, we see that Christ brought them also to *an understanding of their situation.* In these chapters we have seen Jesus as the original analyst, the skilled physician who could ask a few searching questions that compelled a man to face the truth about himself. A wise analyst encourages a patient to talk himself out, to think through his problems, to examine all the factors and arrive at a new understanding of his situation. Christ did that for Cleopas and his companion. He asked them one leading question: "Was it not necessary that the Christ should suffer these things and enter into his glory?" Then, recalling for them the Old Testament prophecies, deeply rooted in their minds, he showed them the death of their Master as a part of God's great redemptive plan. We can see the fog beginning to lift as they talked with this sympathetic stranger, almost as though they realized how groundless and unreasonable and unnecessary was their melancholy mood. Later they described the experience to each other, "Did not our hearts burn within us while he talked to us on the road . . .?"

The writer of the forty-second Psalm plumbed the depths of despair. His spirits sank so low that he wept as only a strong man can weep. Taunted by his pagan enemies, he cried out, "My tears have been my meat day and night, while they continually say unto me, Where is thy God?" But this Hebrew poet also possessed a remarkable insight into his total situation. With keen powers of self-analysis he looked at himself, at what he had been and at what he might become, and exclaimed in faith, "Why art thou cast down, O my soul? and why art thou disquieted within me? hope thou in God; for I shall yet praise him, who is the health of my countenance and my God." He was saying to himself what Christ said to the two disciples: God still reigns. He has all things in control.

Even this tragedy which has crushed your spirit fits into his plan. It will pass, and you will again have cause to praise him.

That becomes our essential situation when we encounter the God who revealed himself in Christ and that will be the hope that rescues us from the slough of despond. The Apostle Paul was no stranger to the mood of depression. Writing of his afflictions, he said, "We were so utterly, unbearably crushed that we despaired of life itself." But one thing kept Paul on his feet. Conjuring up the worst calamities that could happen to him, all the enemies of the human soul, all the demonic forces in this universe, he dared them to do their damnedest, declaring, "If God be for us, who can be against us? He that spared not his own Son, but delivered him up for us all, how shall he not with him also freely give us all things?"

It is the essential situation of every believing Christian. Reading some of the letters which leaders of the German Resistance Movement wrote from Hitler's concentration camps, we are struck not only by their absence of despondency but by their mood of quiet joy. One prisoner, before being executed, wrote to his family:

"My mood has often vacillated between hope and the most gloomy anticipation. But on one point my state of mind has remained constant, serene and firm. I have resigned myself unconditionally to the will of God. Not once have I been assailed by any doubt that what God wills even in this situation is just and good. Not for one moment have I contended with *him*. Therefore, despite some very gloomy hours, despair has remained far from me." Then he adds, "Strange as it may sound, I have learned one thing in prison — to be joyful."*

The greatest thing that Christ did for the despondent pair on the Emmaus Road was to give them *reason for a new joy*. At their home in Emmaus he joined them for supper, assumed

* *Dying We Live*, ed. by Helmut Golliwitzer, Kathe Kuhn, Reinhold Schneider; translated by Reinhard C. Kuhn (Pantheon Books Inc., New York, 1956; Harvill Press, London).

the role of host, took bread, blessed and broke it and in this sacramental gesture disclosed himself as their familiar Friend. Luke tells us, "Their eyes were opened and they recognized him." This was the totally new and unexpected factor which entered their situation, the factor of which they had heard rumours but which they had not dared to believe. While they mourned the crucified Jesus, the risen Christ encountered them and walked beside them on their sorrowful journey. He rescued them from the slough of despond by undergirding them with his own re-enforcing presence.

Nothing in life so lifts our spirits as the presence of some strong, buoyant personality. I once knew a man who was more than a man; he was like the shadow of a great rock in a weary land. He breathed reassurance. However gloomy and dark your situation, the moment he entered it the clouds began to break. He had a favourite expression, "It will emerge", and he always left you with a new heart, feeling that in God's time a solution would indeed emerge. With him you could honestly believe the promise of scripture that "weeping may endure for a night, but joy cometh in the morning".

This is the joy of Easter—the glorious good news that beside us at all times on life's journey there is a Presence who lifts our gloom as he lifted the gloom of the two disciples on the road to Emmaus. Some years ago I read an unsophisticated book by Charles M. Sheldon entitled *He is Here*. The author pictures Christ coming to a number of people who are being sorely tested and giving them strength and courage according to their need. A brilliant surgeon, ready to operate on a critically injured man, is completely unnerved when he recognizes the patient as his own estranged and dissolute son. For a moment the surgeon seems about to collapse, but then a Presence makes itself felt, calming his heart, steadying his hand and restoring his magic skill. An underpaid shop clerk verges towards suicide, because her evenings are made bitter by the constant carping of a selfish, invalid mother, and her days made hopeless through the dreary, unrewarding work at the shop. Just as she reaches the end of her rope a Stranger leans over the counter and speaks a few reassuring words that give her the strength to keep going. So the story continues with incident after incident of the re-enforcing Presence coming to beaten, bullied and whipped men and women, lifting their depressed spirits and imparting to them the resources to carry on.

This is not fiction but fact, validated in the lives of all the great Christians, as true for us now as it was for the disciples on the evening of the first Easter Day. It need not be a mystical experience, a hand on the shoulder, a voice from the unseen, a vision in the night, but simply our firm belief in Christ's own promise, "Lo, I am with you always, even to the end of the world." To believing men and women Christ comes in the unshakable assurance that they are not alone, that beside them on the road there is one who can help because he has walked that road before them. To such people Christ is as real as their families and friends. They speak to him, listen to him, consult him and draw their inspiration from him. Upheld by his strong, buoyant, radiant, exuberant spirit, they can never remain trapped for very long in the slough of despond.

But the crucial encounter with Christ does not happen accidentally. We must consciously open our lives to him. Cleopas and his companion testified that Christ made himself known to them "in the breaking of the bread"; and this also has been validated in Christian experience. The lowly Brother Lawrence might find Christ as real in the monastery kitchen as at the high altar, but most Christians would testify that in the sacrament of the breaking of bread they have encountered Christ as in no other way. This is true. Often I have stood in a hospital ward and marvelled at the calm serenity of a patient's face as I touched his lips with the consecrated bread and repeated the words of Jesus, "This is my body . . ." Often I have watched men and women enter the sanctuary with slumped shoulders and downcast eyes, then rise from the sacramental act of worship as though with a new strength and hope. Christ himself has provided the avenues of living encounter in the sacraments, the Bible, prayer and the fellowship of the Church, all those means of grace which recall the memory of his personal ministry upon earth and which open our lives to his continuing ministry here and now. Let us come, then, and let us come often to that place where we may encounter Christ; and, though we have sorrow now, our hearts will rejoice, and no-one will take our joy from us.